TALMUDICAL ACADEMY

Adelphia is . . .

. . . A *Makom Torah* where the Divine Presence is felt as Rabbeim and Talmidim exchange *divrei Torah*, *Chochma*, and *Mussar* in an environment that is most conducive to learning.

. . . A staff of gifted mechanchim that are dedicated to the success of every talmid. A staff that provides hours of individualized attention in helping each talmid develop his potential. A staff that has the unique ability to kindle the flame of Torah and Yiddishkeit while responding as each new challenge arises.

. . . A place which all talmidim, past and present, lovingly think of as their second home. A place where alumni return for *Yomim Tovim*, simchos and other special occasions and feel comfortable "dropping in" at almost any time for advice, divrei chizuk, or just a friendly chat.

It is in these elements which we at the Yeshiva take pride and which account for our unusual success. Our success, however, would not be possible without the enthusiastic support we have received from parents, alumni and other friends. To you we express our heartfelt appreciation.

It is with special thanks to Hashem for our past accomplishments that we offer our fervent prayer that we be deemed worthy of continuing this great work in the future.

ADELPHIA, NEW JERSEY

THE BOOK OF
OUR HERITAGE

Eliyahu Kitov

THE BOOK OF OUR HERITAGE

The Jewish year and its days of significance

SPECIAL EDITION

Shavuos

Translated from the Hebrew SEFER HA-TODA'AH
by NATHAN BULMAN

Revised by Dovid Landesman

FELDHEIM PUBLISHERS

Jerusalem / New York

ISBN — 0-87306-728-2

FELDHEIM PUBLISHERS
POB 35002 / Jerusalem, Israel

200 Airport Executive Park
Nanuet, N.Y. 10954

Printed and bound in U.S.A. by
Noble Book Press Corp.
New York, NY 10001

CONTENTS

Ruth and David

CHAPTER ONE

RUTH

Our Sages noted: This *megillah* [Ruth] does not include laws of purity or defilement, prohibitions or permitted acts. Why then was it written? To teach you the reward due those who perform acts of kindness (*Yalkut Shimoni* 601).

The statement bears examination, for there are many essential mitzvos and laws which we derive from this *megillah* — laws pertaining to converts, laws dealing with gifts that are to be disbursed to the poor, laws of modesty as well as numerous others. All of them are deduced from Ruth and from her exemplary behavior. Yet, the Sages question why this *megillah* was recorded!

Had Ruth not possessed a singularly outstanding quality that all of us should evidence and which is worthy of study so that we might emulate her behavior, the other qualities that we see in her would have never developed.

Indeed, most converts contribute little to Israel and are even seen as potentially problematic, for they bring with them forms of behavior and attitudes which have no place in God's assembly. Whatever fine qualities that converts evidence are based on what they learn from Israel. The community of Israel has no lack of scholars and righteous people that would force us to turn to converts to teach us what is prohibited and what is forbidden, what is pure and what is defiled, what constitutes thievery and cheating, or to demonstrate modesty or proper social behavior!

Ruth embodied a character trait in which Israel was deficient in

9

that period — a quality that was temporarily missing in the nation's collective nature. It was this quality that Ruth contributed to the body of Israel. By virtue of this quality she merited that Israel learned many other additional traits and laws by studying her behavior — even though these laws and traits are part and parcel of Israel's psyche.

Ruth's outstanding quality was her kindness. So refined was her kindness that she was able to absorb all other fine character traits and obligations — inculcating them at once when she joined Israel. Although she absorbed all of her other qualities and the laws which she fulfilled when she joined Israel, her kindness brought her the merit that enabled her to become the role model who would teach others.

AN AMONITE AND MOABITE SHALL NOT ENTER THE ASSEMBLY OF GOD

No other people are as abhorred and as distinctly different from Israel than are these two nations — especially Moav.

The Torah (*Devarim* 23:8) teaches us: YOU SHALL NOT DESPISE EDOM even though they seized every opportunity to attempt to destroy Israel. When Edom was unable to personally inflict harm upon Israel, they joyously watched as others plundered Israel's wealth. Edom was the progenitor of Amalek — Israel's most vicious enemy throughout history. We may do battle with them, subjugate them, even annihilate them — but we are proscribed from abhorring them. Why? BECAUSE THEY ARE YOUR BROTHERS (ibid.). Internecine hatred has one limit — abhorrence! Should one of them seek to join his fate with yours, draw him near, for by coming to you he seeks to return to your common roots. Wait three generations until his hatred dissipates and then he may enter your assembly.

YOU SHALL NOT DEPISE EGYPT (ibid.) even though they are the most contaminated of nations, even though they were the first to subjugate, afflict and humiliate Israel. They cast your sons into the river — some they slaughtered and some they strangled. They made your life bitter, yet you may not despise them, for YOU WERE A STRANGER IN THEIR LAND (ibid.). A place to rest is a refuge — even if the conditions are oppressive! If someone provides you with shelter when you are in need — you owe them your very life! The obligation to be grateful has no bounds. Thus, should one of them seek to join his fate with yours, remember how his forefathers welcomed you into their land. Wait for three generations until his contaminated character vanishes and then repay him in the greatest way possible — accept him into your assembly.

However, AN AMONITE OR MOABITE SHALL NOT ENTER THE ASSEMBLY OF GOD. EVEN THE TENTH GENERATION SHALL NOT ENTER UNTO ETERNITY (ibid. :4). They were not as wicked as Edom nor as defiled as Egypt, yet we are dutybound to abhor them. Even if one of them might attempt to join you, he will despise you forever. He can never be purified of his defilement; therefore distance yourself from him and do not accept him.

In what way was their sin greater than others? War and murder are not abhorrent acts among the nations of the world. Indeed, hatred and impurity flow through the veins of nations throughout history. As long as the Master of the World has not wiped them out we may not despise them. They have honor and we must accord them respect, for they all have at least one redeeming quality. Even if today they attempt to destroy you — tomorrow they might smile and act kindly. Amon and Moav, on the other hand, are the embodiment of ingratitude and they are incapable of acting kindly.

They are not your brothers, but they grew up in your father's household. In Abraham's merit they were saved from the conflagration that destroyed Sodom and became nations in their own right. At least once in their history they should have provided you with a meager portion of bread and a flask of water — given it to you not because you were in need but because of the respect which they owed your forefather. When you were on your way out of Egypt they should have done so. Even if they would have later attacked you it would be understandable, for this is the way in which all nations act.

Amon and Moav did not moblilize their forces to wage war with you. They knew that they were incapable of doing so, but they still showed their denigrated essence. FOR THEY DID NOT GREET YOU WITH BREAD AND WATER WHEN YOU WERE ON YOUR WAY OUT OF EGYPT (ibid. :5). They are abominable ingrates; their nature is more debased than that of a murderer! The latter acts out of the passions of his heart, and a heart that is passionate can become compassionate. Worst of all is he who has no heart, for he can never perform an act of kindness. These nations are therefore to be estranged forever, for the very foundation of the world is kindness.

Moav's villiany was even greater than that of Amon. MY NATION! REMEMBER THE DESIGNS OF BALAK, KING OF MOAV (Michah 6:5). FOR HE HIRED BIL'AM BEN BE'OR OF PESOR ARAM NAHARAYIM TO CURSE YOU (Devarim 23:5). As a nation, they were given a sword — to live by or to die by. And if they lacked courage and feared war — they should have opened their treasury and hired mercenaries to fight their battles. But they did neither. Instead, they sought to destroy an entire people by hiring a drunkard for a niggardly sum, asking him to place a curse upon you. And whom did they seek to curse? The nation that brings bounty to the world, that is the source of blessing for all nations. Avaricious as they were, Moav carefully guarded their funds. But for the nation to whom they owed their very existence they had no mercy. Let their seed never be mixed with yours!

Balak, the parsimonious ingrate who was their ruler, had a son whose name was Eglon. Like his father, he was a miser and felt no debt of gratitude. To Eglon a daughter was born whose name was Ruth. Ruth — princess of Moav — what was she like?

AVRAHAM'S KINDNESS

Avraham was unique, for in the merit of his kindness and benevolence the entire world was saved from the Divine wrath aroused by the evil prevalent in his time. Avraham journeyed throughout the area and in every place where he dwelled, he spread kindness and benevolence, influencing others and teaching them to emulate his traits. Lot, his nephew, accompanied him everywhere.

The years passed by and his efforts seemed to have been in vain — he had performed numerous acts of kindness but there was no one who followed his path. Where were all of those whom he had trained? Even Lot, his nephew, had left his side to settle in Sodom.

But Avraham did not abandon his efforts. He was willing to wait even four hundred years to see the tangible manifestations of his teachings. Through his son Yitzchak he began once again to build a people and nation within whom Divine kindness would be evident in every action and from among whom it would never disappear.

The nation was formed and God took them out of Egypt and brought them to the boundary of His holiness. Avraham's kindness was now embodied in an entire people and they had inherited a land which they were about to make their own.

And within this nation, who was to stand at the head of the people as they took possession of their land? He whose kindness was greater than all of his brothers, he who was incapable of being ungrateful, he who was willing to condemn himself and justify others. Indeed, his very name bespeaks kindness and thanksgiving. He was to lead his brothers into the land, standing at their head as they followed. AND GOD SAID: YEHUDAH SHALL LEAD (*Shoftim* 1:2).

Who were the elect members of the tribe of Yehudah? The residents of Beis Lechem, for Beis Lechem was like the home of Avraham; he who entered its environs hungry, left completely sated. And who was the leading citizen of Beis Lechem? It was Elimelech, son of Nachson ben Aminadav, like his father prince of the tribe of Yehudah and leader of his generation.

AND THERE WAS FAMINE IN THE LAND (*Ruth* 1:1). The nation, descendents of Avraham, were all in need of kindness. Who would save them in their time of distress? They all looked to the greatest man of the nation, to Elimelech.

AND A MAN WENT FROM BEIS LECHEM IN YEHUDAH (ibid.). Why did Elimelech leave? He said: "Now all of Israel will gather at my door, each one of them with his charity box. I shall leave and escape from them." (*Ruth Rabah* 1)

To where did he flee? TO DWELL IN THE FIELDS OF MOAV (ibid.) — to pitch his tent among the descendents of the man who had left Avraham's home and had established residence in Sodom! It was there that the leader of Avraham's nation fled when his brothers were in need!

Avraham's kindness had been transferred from his tent to a home, from a home to an abode, from an abode to the palace and from the palace to the inner sanctum. And behold, it had but entered the inner sanctum and seemed to have disappeared.

God therefore said: "I decree that the one who is uplifted shall descend and the one who is lowly shall ascend."

14

IN THE FIELDS OF MOAV

God forbid that we infer that kindness had totally disappeared from among Avraham's children. It was still existent within the tents of Israel's tribes in sufficient measure to give viability to each individual household. However, the unique kindness which is the crown of Israel's leadership had proven to be deficient. The unique quality of gratitude, of humility and honesty which brought a previous leader to admit that a certain woman was more righteous than he, that led him to declare, "I shall stand in judgement but let not a fingernail of the innocent be harmed" — this quality was no longer evident in Beis Lechem.

The entire nation was in a state of distress — was Elimelech who had fled in the face of their needs to be permitted to live in luxury?

AND ELIMELECH DIED (ibid 1:2) — God struck him down for having failed to provide for the people. "You were the elect of My nation. Because you caused their hearts to fall, descend!"

AND SHE AND HER TWO SONS WERE LEFT (ibid.) — Naomi and two orphans, on their own in the fields of Moav. In this very same field of Moav there were two young women — also orphans, for Ehud had killed their father Eglon and another had usurped his throne. Having fallen from their previous state, they were married off to Elimelech's two sons who had also fallen from their previous stature.

The father, Elimelch, had never intended to emigrate to Moav but only to live there temporarily. Once he died, his sons said: "We shall dwell in the fields of Moav — not as strangers but as citizens." AND THEY MARRIED MOABITE WOMEN AND THEY LIVED THERE FOR TEN YEARS (ibid.).

The women did not become Jewesses. Their husbands sought to become citizens of Moav — why would their wives convert?

Moreover, could Moabite women be accepted as converts? The Torah taught to them in Beis Lechem categorically stated that AN AMONITE AND MOABITE SHALL NOT ENTER THE ASSEMBLY OF GOD, FOR THEY DID NOT WELCOME YOU WITH BREAD AND WATER.

Was there any piety to be found among the daughters of that land? Could there be even a modicum of modesty in a nation descended from a mother who named her child Moav — you are my son from my father! Could the homes that they established with husbands who abandoned their people to emigrate to Moav be any better than the other households of Moav? There was within them no desire to convert, no piety nor modesty — there was no comparison between them and the homes of Beis Lechem in Yehudah. They lived in THE FIELDS OF MOAV — in a place that was desolate and inappropriate for the growth of those who were the fruits of Beis Lechem.

Nevertheless, there was one gem waiting to be found there — a jewel that would only be found once its previous owner had totally abandoned hope of ever recovering it. The gem had been lost by its original owner and had rolled through the refuse of Sodom, ending up in Moav. When the heirs of the original owner abandoned hope of rediscovering the gem, then it would be found.

AND BOTH MACHLON AND CHILYON DIED (ibid.) — he [Elimelech] who had previously been above the rest was now completely denigrated. The time had come for the degraded to arise.

MOTHER OF ROYALTY

AND HE [SHLOMO] PLACED A THRONE FOR THE MOTHER OF THE KING (Melachim I 2:19) — R. Elazar explained: MOTHER OF THE KING — this refers to Ruth (Bava Basra 91b).

What characteristic typified this woman that she alone merited to develop the royal line that ruled the children of Avraham, that she was worthy of the title "mother of royalty" of the kingdom of kindness instead of one of Avraham's own daughters?

The answer is that Ruth was the embodiment of the trait of kindness which Avraham had implanted in his nephew Lot, a trait which we might have thought to have disappeared when Lot went to live in Sodom. Lot was the founding father of Moav, a nation that exemplified ingratitude and a total lack of kindness. Nevertheless, there was a remnant of kindness that remained of the kindness which Avraham had sewn.

This trait remained unapparent for some seven hundred years — surviving though it passed through all types of refuse and contamination until it bloomed in Ruth. And when it bloomed, it burst forth in an aura of bright light which no darkness or fog would ever be able to conceal. Let this one — Ruth — come forth and heal one of the descendents of Avraham who had grown up in his house but had nevertheless been infected with an unwillingness to share his bread. Let Ruth, this spiritual descendent of Avraham who came from outside of his household but who had withstood all of the trials and tribulations, come and heal the descendent who had grown up in Avraham's home but had failed when tested.

This was the plan of the One whose counsel is hidden. Let the remedy for the malady of his select son come from the most denigrated of his enemies and from the most insignificant of places. The remedy did not constitute use of foreign elements. Rather, both the person who brought the cure and the one who suffered from the malady stemmed from the same origin. The remedy also had her roots in Beis Lechem, but her trait had been hidden in captivity and was only now free to return to its original source.

THE KINGDOM OF YEHUDAH

God made Israel into a kingdom of *kohanim* and chose one household among them in whose hands the scepter of royalty was to be eternally placed. He did not do so because His world was deficient in either kingdoms or kings. Rather, He had ordained in His wisdom that there was to be one kingdom on earth that would correspond to His ethereal kingdom.

Of the kingdom of heaven it is said: Anywhere where you see evidence of His grandeur, there you see evidence of His humility. The kingdom which the Master of the Earth came to establish was to share this quality; a kingdom of truth in which grandeur and humility would coexist and serve simultaneously.

Grandeur that does not evidence humility is debasement. Man, you are but one element within creation — what right do you have to be haughty? If the Creator chose to bestow an abundant measure of His kindness upon you, then you are dutybound to feel even more humility and gratitude! If you fail to give thanks and recognize His goodness, then you are the most debased of all — a Sodomite, an Amonite and a Moabite!

By the same token, humility which denies grandeur is conceit. The Creator has imparted within you elements of His kindness and goodness and has granted you greatness. Why do you reject His gift? Even if you are lowly in comparison to those greater than you, you still have a great measure of His goodness within you. If you come to give thanks, you are dutybound to recognize this gift first. Do not say "I am debased" and therefore not obligated to express thanks, for by doing so you reject His gift and show your conceit!

Wherever you find greatness, humility must be there as well and vice versa. A kingdom can not be complete unless it evidences both of these qualities to the ultimate degree. If the sovereignty has no peer in grandeur, than it must also have no peer in humility — this alone is the sign of true royalty. Has such an earthly kingdom ever been established by mortal man?

This was the type of kingdom that God said that he would establish in Israel and it was this kingdom that Ruth became mother to, for she RETURNED FROM THE FIELDS OF MOAV (Ruth 1:6). She RETURNED to her exalted roots — this was her grandeur; FROM THE FIELDS OF MOAV — this was her humility.

RUTH'S KINDNESS

Scripture refers to two acts of kindness that Ruth showed in her relationship with her mother-in-law. The second act of kindness was greater than the first — SHE DID NOT FOLLOW THE YOUNG MEN, NEITHER RICH NOR POOR (ibid. 3:10).

The ten years that Ruth spent in her mother-in-law Naomi's home were all equally good. Ruth brought Naomi no grief. Rather, she made every effort to bring joy to the heart of the widow who had fallen from greatness until Ruth herself was widowed. But all of her previous acts of kindness are not recorded, for they are overshadowed by the kindness that she showed then. Ruth's first acts of kindness could have been performed by anyone. Even a person who is wrapped up in his own life occasionally sees the anguish of others and is moved to show compassion.

The first recorded act of kindness toward Naomi transpired after the death of Ruth's husband and it typifies the unique kindness that is the trait of Avraham. We are told of a person who forgets her own troubles and anguish and concerns herself completely with the needs of another. When Ruth comes to act kindly toward her mother-in-law, she does so without reservation and without any thought about her own needs. This was the kindness that Ruth performed toward Naomi AFTER THE DEATH OF HER HUSBAND (ibid. 1:3); i.e., when she herself was in need of comfort and solace. She did not simply act kindly toward Naomi — she transformed herself into a source of kindness, giving to Naomi without leaving anything for herself.

This kindness was outweighed by the second act, for later Ruth gave Naomi more than she had herself. She transformed herself into a new being solely for Naomi's benefit. Ruth saw that all that she had been was insufficient to fill the needs of Naomi. What did Ruth do? Ruth clothed herself in royalty AND WENT TO BOAZ AS HER MOTHER-IN LAW HAD COMMANDED (ibid. 3:6). Let us examine the acts of kindness to which Scripture refers.

I AM ENTIRELY YOURS

Ruth, daughter of Eglon king of Moav, had wed the son of a foreign nation — a man from Beis Lechem. For ten years she lived with this stranger and knew no happiness. All of the dreams of her youth had faded and now this man was dead. Would it not have been understandable had she now chosen to seek her happiness among her own people? She was still young and beautiful and all of the nobles and rich men of the land sought her company.

But she said to herself: "This poor woman — Naomi, my mother-in-law — what is to become of her? I did not bring her to this land. She came with her husband and two sons. She was wealthy when she came — with an honored husband and sons ready to start their own families. Her past was proud and her future seemed bright. Merciful God! How bereft is this poor woman now. I can not allow her to return to her nation empty-handed.

"But what can you return to her that she has lost? You can not revive her husband or bring her sons back to life! Nor can you return her youth. A calamity has struck her and you are not its cause. What can you offer her?

"I have nothing to give her that will replace what she has lost. I can only give her myself and revive her soul.

"But you are a Moabite, and Naomi is returning to Beis Lechem. When you accompany her there, you will be a bitter reminder of her disgrace and guilt and will be denigrated by all her people, for you are the source of her humiliation! Why should you add grief to her anguish?

"But as of now, and until death tears us apart, I am no longer a Moabite. I am the daughter of Naomi — I have no other parents. I have no homeland and no people, no other life or death other than with Naomi. Her people is my people, her God is my God. Whatever my mother Naomi shall instruct me to do, whatever I shall perceive as being pleasing to her, that I shall do. I am not the daughter of a strange god nor am I a convert. From the depth of my being until my dying day I am completely hers.

"I am so close to Naomi, so drawn to her, that no one can cause us to part. I have abandoned the royal house of Moav to travel to Beis Lechem, to serve there as a simple maidservant so as to pay honor to her God and her people. Who could find cause to humiliate Naomi because of me?"

AND FOR YOUR SAKE I SHALL CLOTHE MYSELF IN ROYALTY

When Ruth decided to accompany Naomi to live amongst a people she did not know, she sought only to be treated as a simple maidservant waiting on her mistress. When her mistress would die her life would end as well, for she had no other reason to live other than to serve Naomi. She never thought that she would marry a man in Beis Lechem from the tribe of Yehudah. She was a Moabite — who would destroy his seed by taking her? The verse states: AN AMONITE AND MOABITE SHALL NOT ENTER THE ASSEMBLY OF GOD ETERNALLY. The prohibition would not seem to differentiate between men and women, just as the prohibition of accepting an Edomite, an Egyptian or a *mamzer* does not differentiate between men and women.

But the Holy One, blessed is He, who is the creator of the light of *mashiach,* had a different plan. In the first generations after the Torah was given, the question was never posed as to whether the prohibition of allowing an Amonite to be accepted included both men and women. The halachah was never taught and thus no tradition existed, for there had never been a need to issue a public ruling. There had never been a single Moabite who was worthy of being included in the assembly of God. It was only in the generation of Boaz and Ruth that the question arose. It was then that the Sages sat and concluded that the Torah spoke of AN AMONITE and not an Amonitess, of A MOABITE and not a Moabitess. Should one ask that the Torah also employs the male form for Edomites, Egyptians and *mamzerim* even though those proscriptions apply to females as well, the prohibition referring to Amon and Moav differs, for the Torah includes a reason for the prohibition. BECAUSE THEY DID NOT WELCOME YOU WITH BREAD AND WATER (*Devarim* 23:5) — this claim could not be applied to females, for it is unnatural for women to provide passersby with provisions. On the other hand, the prohibition of allowing an Edomite or Egyptian [for three generations] and a *mamzer* [forever] has no accompanying reason provided and applies to men and women equally.

In the generation of Boaz, God illuminated the eyes of the Sages who elucidated this halachah, for it was then that it had practical application. The community of Israel waited for Ruth to RETURN FROM THE FIELDS OF MOAV so that the light of *mashiach* might be revealed through her.

When Ruth joined the assembly of God, this halachah was once again forgotten by many of the Sages and doubt began to arise in this matter. This doubt, which persisted in subsequent generations in the minds of the Sages, was also part of the Divine plan, for the door was not to be left open for all Moabite women who sought to join God's assembly. Moreover, there was another secret reason which was to only be revealed when the time had arrived to allow the light of *mashiach* to be revealed in its full majesty. The *mashiach* was to first pass through stages of trepidation and fear. The path of the anointed king — David — was to be paved with two extremes: abysmal depths on one hand and Heavenly heights leading to the celestial throne on the other.

This is what God's wisdom had ordained. The path taken by the anointed king was to be paved in both grandeur and humility — grandeur without peer and humility without comparison. The gates of Torah wisdom and the depths of its truth were opened to the Sages for Ruth's benefit so that she might be wed to Boaz. Boaz was the head of the *sanhedrin* and leader of Israel after Elimelech's death. His greatness was revealed — a foundation of sovereignty. Ruth — a Moabite convert who came to gather sheaves after the reapers — was the embodiment of humility, another of the foundations of sovereignty. The Holy One, blessed is He, who knows the secrets of the heart, perceived the concurrent concealed sides of their characters — the humility of Boaz and the grandeur of Ruth.

When two spiritual giants are joined, what is their issue? A hero of epic proportion. Boaz wed Ruth and David was their descendant. David, of whom the verse states: SKILLED IN PERFORMING, A MAN OF VALOR, A WARRIOR, PERCEPTIVE, A MAN OF CHARACTER AND GOD IS WITH HIM (*Shmuel* I 16:18). SKILLED IN PERFORMING — in his knowledge of *mikra* [the written Torah]. A MAN OF VALOR — in his knowledge of *mishnah* [the orally transmitted Torah]. A WARRIOR — in knowing how to negotiate the battle of Torah. PERCEPTIVE — in his good deeds. A MAN OF CHARACTER — in Talmud, for he made the halachah clear. AND GOD IS WITH HIM — for the halachah is decided in accordance with his opinion (Ruth Rabbah 4).

Naomi merited that her intentions coincided with the Divine plan. After Ruth became her daughter, she sent her to Boaz so that sovereignty might not depart from her house. Ruth would have never considered it possible that she was about to inherit the most precious of Israel's crowns. Given her humility, she would have been content to marry a poor and obscure young man and would have felt incapable of sufficiently expressing her gratitude for for having merited becoming part of God's inheritance. She surely could not see herself as reaching the highest plateau possible. Ruth would have naturally sought to escape from grandeur, but she did not, for she said: "I am now the daughter of Naomi. Let me restore grandeur to its rightful place. All that I am is Naomi's. Even those traits that are naturally mine, I shall make part of me. For Naomi's sake I shall even dress myself in royalty, for ALL THAT YOU SAY TO ME I SHALL DO (Ruth 1:5). "

DAVID — THE SON OF RUTH

What does the name Ruth connote? R. Yochanan explained: That she merited that her descendent was David who sated God with his songs and praise [the name Ruth is etymologically similar to the Hebrew riva — satiated] (Berachos 7b). God, as it were, thirsted for song and praise and and there was no one who could quench this thirst until David came and sated it.

The upshot of this statement is that David's ability existed in potential in Ruth and it was for this reason that she was given a name which etymologically signifies that God would be sated with praise. Three generations passed between Ruth and David — Ruth gave birth to Oved who gave birth to Yishai who gave birth to David. David was Yishai's eighth son and it was only he who expressed the potential that her name signified. In his songs of praise to God he expressed his recognition of her role — GIVE STRENGTH TO YOUR SERVANT AND SAVE THE SON OF YOUR MAIDSERVANT (Tehillim 86:16), I AM YOUR SERVANT, THE SON OF YOUR MAIDSERVANT (ibid. 116:16). David was well aware of Ruth's contribution to his ability. God had revealed it to him when He said: ASK OF ME AND I SHALL GRANT NATIONS AS YOUR INHERITANCE (ibid. 2:8). If they are evil and rebellious, then YOU SHALL BREAK THEM WITH AN IRON ROD (ibid. :9). But if they are good and honest, then teach them to sing with you — PRAISE GOD ALL NATIONS, LAUD HIM ALL PEOPLES (ibid. 117:1).

All of the souls whom Avraham had drawn close to God, could now arise and give praise. Avraham was the first of the seven shepherds whom God placed in this world, and as FATHER TO A MULTITUDE OF NATIONS (Bereishis 17:5), taught the way of God. And now God brought the seventh shepherd — David — to judge the nations as His anointed, raising them to the level wherein NO NATION WILL LIFT A SWORD AGAINST ANOTHER NATION AND THEY WILL NO LONGER LEARN WAR (Yeshayahu 2:4) and ALL SOULS WILL PRAISE GOD (Tehillim 150:6). Avraham had begun the mission of drawing mankind close to the Divine presence and though they had distanced themselves through the ages, David would draw them back and they would never again leave. David knew that this ability came to him through Ruth and he therefore characterized himself as I AM YOUR SERVANT, THE SON OF YOUR MAIDSERVANT (ibid. 116:16).

THE SONG OF THE TORAH

Our Sages taught: David was born on Shavuos and died on Shavuos — i.e., on the sixth of Sivan, the day on which the Torah was given. On the day of the receiving of the Torah, David's sun rose. Seventy years passed, David "received the Torah" seventy-one times and his sun set on the day of the receiving of the Torah and he was gathered unto his people. Just as his birth and passing are inextricably linked to the Torah, so too was his entire life and all of his songs and praise linked to Torah.

The Torah has many different facets. Avraham found within the Torah the aspect of fulfilling the mitzvos which the Master of Kindness ordained upon those who benefit from His kindness. The souls who he drew close to God followed the path he charted but later strayed.

Moshe and his generation found the aspect of fearing God by virtue of the Divine presence and awesome miracles which God performed before the eyes of the entire world. The leaders of the nations were confused and were seized by trembling — but they did not accept the Torah.

David found within the Torah the aspect of song. And when the son of David shall come at the end of days, all of the nations of the world will be gathered to him and will crown God as sovereign.

Rambam (*Hilchos Teshuvah 9*) writes:

> For the king who shall arise from the seed of David will be wiser than Shlomo and a prophet almost as great as Moshe. He will thus be able to teach the entire nation and show them the way of God. And all nations will come to hear him.

The five divisions of *Tehillim* correspond to the five divisions of the Torah. David's songs of praise are a facet of the Torah received at Sinai, for they reveal the aspect of song that is within the Torah. Thus, David himself declared: YOUR STATUTES HAVE BECOME MY SONGS (*Tehillim* 119:54).

Where did David draw the ability to compose these Torah songs? From his mother Ruth, for she had been drowning in the depths of the abyss and had raised herself toward the firmament. David's songs have the same power, for they speak to man in all situations — from one who has sunk to the lowest depths until he who perceives the aura of the Divine throne and all that is in between.

A DEEP SECRET

Ruth's secret potential — the satiating songs and praise of the entire Torah — was hidden from her contemporaries, even after they recalled that the halachah ordained that a Moabite was proscribed but not a Moabitess. Boaz's uncle was still reluctant to take her as a wife, for he feared LEST I DESTROY MY INHERITANCE (*Ruth* 4:6). There were people who never doubted the truth of the halachah but still doubted the wisdom of Boaz's action. They said: "She is a Moabite. Even if she is permitted to join the assembly, is it necessary that she be raised until the house of Boaz — the household which is most consecrated for the Kingdom of Heaven!?"

Our Sages taught: The very night when Boaz took Ruth into his home was his last night. The next morning all arose to attend his funeral. The One whose counsel is hidden had a deep purpose in this matter. Boaz's lifespan had not been prerecorded in the Book of Life. God kept him among the living until Boaz would implant his seed in Ruth so as to give rise to David who was the descendent of these two spiritual giants. When Boaz had fulfilled the Divine will, he departed from the world.

However, we can imagine the inner thoughts of many of the people who witnessed what transpired. Any who were mistaken could interpret what had happened as being a revelation of Divine displeasure with Boaz for having defiled his family. Had not Elimelech, Boaz's uncle, been punished along with his two sons for the very same sin — defiling their families with the seed of Moav?

Many said to themselves: "At least let no child be born from this union!" But God was waiting impatiently, as it were, for this child. When a son was born to Ruth, we do not find Scripture telling us of great public joy that a son had been born to the leader of the generation. Only Naomi's neighbors expressed happiness and it was they who give the child his name. Where were the leading citizens and elders of the city who had given their blessing to Boaz beforehand? Perhaps they too were puzzled by Boaz's sudden death after his union with Ruth? Perhaps they began to wonder if they had not been mistaken when they had ruled that a Moabitess was permitted and the union was therefore suspect?

Because Naomi's neighbors took care of Ruth and her son and offered their blessings, God invested their words with holiness and made them part of the Torah, permanently recording them in *Megillas Ruth*. AND THE NEIGHBORS THERE CALLED HIM A NAME, DECLARING: A SON HAS BEEN BORN TO NAOMI. AND THEY CALLED HIS NAME OVED, HE IS THE FATHER OF YISHAI THE FATHER OF DAVID (*Ruth* 4:17).

As noted, the verse is a quote of the words of the neighbors. Why does the verse repeat the fact that the neighbors gave the child his name — AND THE NEIGHBORS THERE CALLED HIM A NAME and THEY CALLED HIS NAME? Furthermore, whenever the Torah uses the term DECLARING in reference to the giving of a name, the term follows the name itself. In this verse, however, Scripture simply notes that they declared A SON HAS BEEN BORN TO NAOMI without telling us the name. Moreover, the verse tells us that they called him OVED but does not explain why he was given this name. The most perplexing part of the verse is its final phrase — HE IS THE FATHER OF YISHAI, THE FATHER OF DA-

VID. If the aim of Scripture is to provide us with David's geneology, the next verse does so more comprehensively for it traces his ancestry all the way back to Peretz the son of Yehudah. Why does this verse give us a shorter version first?

Our Sages explained the verse in the following manner: AND THE NEIGHBORS THERE CALLED HIM A NAME — with reference to this child who stemmed from a Moabite and whose purity was suspect. DECLARING: A SON HAS BEEN BORN TO NAOMI — this child is not to be seen as being the son of a Moabite. He is the seed of Naomi, herself a scion of the most noble family in Yehudah, a grandaughter of Nachshon ben Aminadav, prince of the tribe. AND THEY CALLED HIS NAME OVED — his name is an acronym for *od ben David* — another son and then David. HE IS THE FATHER OF YISHAI THE FATHER OF DAVID — this final phrase was prophecy which God placed in their mouths. It was as if God had said: "May your words [another son and then David] be true."

POVERTY AND SUFFERING

The Sages ask: Why is *Megillas Ruth* read on Shavuos? To teach us that the Torah can only be acquired through poverty and suffering (*Yalkut Shimoni*).

In the same vein one could also explain that this is the reason why David is mentioned in *Megillas Ruth* which is read on Shavuos. This teaches us that one can only become a vehicle of the Kingdom of Heaven on earth through poverty and suffering. Ruth and David shared the same path of affliction.

Who was David? He was the greatest of kings, the most pious of men, the wisest of people, the most humble among the modest and the most glorious of poets who sang before God. Notwithstanding all of this, no one suffered as much anguish in his life as did David. From birth he suffered and his afflictions did not leave him until his very last day when his son Shlomo succeeded him. It was only then that the world came to recognize his greatness, that his enemies were finally silenced.

David himself testified as to his anguish. SAVE ME GOD, FOR THE WATERS [THAT THREATEN TO DROWN ME] HAVE REACHED MY SOUL (*Tehillim* 69:2). The verse, and the ones that follow, reveal great anguish. They can not be seen as mere figures of speech, for only one who is devoid of fear of heaven speaks figuratively before God. Is it possible that David who always justified God's actions and went beyond the requirements of the law would exaggerate his pain when crying out to God for salvation? God forbid that we should think this to be so. Rather, the waters really did reach his soul! Why was his anguish so great?

THOSE WHO HATE ME FOR NO REASON ARE MORE NUMEROUS THAN THE HAIRS OF MY HEAD (ibid. :5). A man has tens of thousands of hairs on his head. Yet David claimed that his enemies were even more numerous! To whom did David do wrong? He showed extraordinary compassion toward Shaul who attempted to kill him! Surely he was merciful toward those who did him no harm! David's kindness toward his fellowman overflowed. Why was he hated?

EVEN THAT WHICH I DID NOT STEAL, I THEN RETURNED (ibid.). The Torah can be interpreted on many levels — literally, allegorically, figuratively and mystically. LIKE A HAMMER WHICH STRIKES STONE (*Yirmiyahu* 23:29), shattering it and spreading shards in all directions, so too the words of Torah can be understood in various ways. This statement can be understood as a reference to Israel's situation among the nations, wherein she stands accused by them of crimes that she has never committed. Nevertheless, the verse has literal meaning that can not be ignored. David was unjustly accused of theft and gave recompense though he had not stolen! How are we to understand what happened?

GOD, YOU [ALONE] ARE AWARE OF MY WRONGDOING AND GUILT. FROM YOU THEY ARE NOT HIDDEN (*Tehillim* 69:6). Was there no one else — not a friend or companion, brother or relative who was aware of David's innocence, who would come forth to testify that he was not evil, that all of the accusations were baseless?

LET THOSE WHO PLACE THEIR TRUST IN YOU NOT BE EMBARRASED BY ME ... FOR YOUR SAKE I HAVE BORNE SHAME (ibid. :7-8). What type of shame did David bear that he considered it to be for God's sake?

I WAS STRANGE TO MY BROTHERS, AN ALIEN TO THE CHILDREN OF MY MOTHER (:9). This verse must also be understood on the literal level and expresses the greatest anguish that a person can feel. A person grows up among brothers and sisters and dwells together with them under the same roof. All of them evidence a close and warm relationship with one another — save for one who is considered to be a stranger in the house and alien to them. Moreover, he is not a real stranger or alien to whom people show some tolerance. Rather, he is a brother — their own flesh and blood — whom they have estranged. [The Hebrew *muzar*, which the psalmist uses in this verse, expresses estrangement on the part of those who relate to him rather than estrangement that is a result of his indeed being a stranger.] He had become a thorn in their sides. When they came in they saw him, when they left they saw him. The point had been reached wherein they could no longer abide his presence. He had been close to them but had nevertheless become estranged from them. Can there be any greater anguish than this? What had David done to deserve this treatment?

FOR THE JEALOUSY OF YOUR HOUSE HAS DEVOURED ME (ibid. :10). Though David refers to YOUR [I.E., GOD'S] HOUSE, the reference is clearly to the house of his father Yishai, for in the entire world there is no other house that was as suitable a dwelling place for the *Shechinah*. This jealousy, which emanated from a house that is compared to God's, could only be jealousy without ulterior motive and which was purely for the sake of heaven. Why then does David decry that he is being devoured by the jealousy which he senses has arisen because God loves him so much and chose him from among his brothers?

AND THE SHAME OF THOSE WHO BLASPHEMED YOU HAS FALLEN UPON ME (ibid.). It is obvious that all of the shame which was heaped upon David was destined for those who blaspheme God. Why then was it first thrust upon David, God's faithful servant?

I CRIED AS MY SOUL FASTED AND THAT WAS A SOURCE OF SHAME FOR ME. I MADE MY CLOTHING SACKCLOTH AND I BECAME AN EXAMPLE [OF RIDICULE] FOR THEM (ibid. :11-12). Neither fasting nor self-affliction managed to cleanse David of the sins which others saw in him. The gates of repentance are never closed in front of anyone who transgresses. Were they closed before David, who never sinned and was God's chosen from among all generations?

THEY WHO SIT AT THE GATE DISCUSS ME (:13). The reference is to the *Sanhedrin* who sat in judgement as to whether David was fit or unfit since he was descended from Ruth. Though the halachah that a Moabitess could be accepted into the assembly had been reintroduced three generations previously, the court once again deliberated upon the question, for perhaps the earlier ruling had been erroneous. The question concerned all of David's brothers, as well as his father Yishai and grandfather Oved. Yet there was no deliberation regarding their genealogical fitness — only that of David!

I AM THE SUBJECT OF THE SONGS OF THOSE WHO DRINK (ibid.). Those who sat in the marketplaces and wasted their time drinking — they too took an interest in David and composed ditties ridiculing him. Master of the world, merciful Father! Why do You do this to Your righteous follower?

There is an additional chapter in Scripture, whose theme is similar, which is also most difficult to understand. However, if we compare the questions that arise there with those that we have posed here, it is possible that we can begin to comprehend the meaning of the events that transpired in David's life.

The verse (*Shmuel* I 16:2) states: AND GOD SAID TO SHMUEL. FILL YOUR HORN WITH OIL AND GO, FOR I HAVE SENT YOU TO THE HOUSE OF YISHAI OF BEIS LECHEM. FOR I HAVE SEEN AMONG HIS SONS A KING — i.e., in God's eyes he is fit, but it will not be apparent to you that he is worthy of becoming king. AND SHMUEL CAME TO BEIS LECHEM AND ALL OF THE ELDERS OF THE CITY TREMBLED WHEN THEY SAW HIM (ibid. :4) for they knew that all of Shmuel's actions were according to Divine command and therefore understood that he must have come to fulfill an important mission.

AND HE SANCTIFIED YISHAI AND HIS SONS AND HE CALLED THEM TO JOIN HIM IN A SACRIFICE (ibid. :5). Shmuel did not know which of the sons would be anointed as king. He therefore invited "all" of the sons. This episode is most perplexing. Would we think that Yishai would leave out one of the sons? Is it possible that a man as righteous as Yishai would simply forget to bring one of his sons? When anyone among Israel comes to perform a mitzvah, he is exceedingly careful to fulfill it optimally even if the mitzvah is incumbent upon everyone and not only upon him. Surely this is true of one as righteous as Yishai, who was about to perform a mitzvah addressed specifically to him, a mitzvah that entailed the selection of one who was to be God's anointed and which all of Israel anticipated. Surely he would be careful to invite "all" of his sons as Shmuel had instructed. Why did he fail to bring David? Moreover, we find that Yishai brought Elihu — who was the youngest of his sons and had been borne to him from another wife — but still failed to bring David who was older than Elihu.

AND YISHAI BROUGHT HIS SEVEN SONS BEFORE SHMUEL. AND
SHMUEL SAID TO YISHAI: GOD HAS NOT CHOSEN [ANY OF] THESE (ibid.
:10). All of the elders of Beis Lechem understood that Shmuel's
arrival was not a trivial matter and they therefore had TREM-
BLED WHEN THEY SAW HIM. Yishai, who knew the real reason
why the prophet had come — for Shmuel had informed him of
the purpose of his mission — surely understood that God's pur-
poe would be realized. Who, then, should have remembered
that there was yet another son in Yishai's house if not Yishai
himself? Even if there had been some reason why he had ne-
glected to bring David earlier, surely he or one of his sons
should have now remembered to do so and should have
sought forgiveness for not having done so immediately. But Yishai did not remember David and neither did David's seven
brothers. It was as if, Heaven forbid, they were content that
God's intent to anoint a king from their household would remain unrealized!

HIS SEVEN SONS — the phrase would seem to emphasize that
these seven [who Yishai brought before Shmuel] were "all" of-
his sons. But he had an eighth son — David!

AND SHMUEL SAID TO YISHAI: ARE THERE NO MORE YOUTHS? AND
HE [YISHAI] REPLIED: THERE IS A LITTLE ONE REMAINING AND HE IS
TENDING THE FLOCKS (ibid. :11). The verse is most puzzling. Yishai
does not apologize to Shmuel for his failure to bring David. He
refers to David as a "little one" though David was twenty-nine
at the time! He then informs Shmuel that David is tending the
flocks as if that made any difference! Moreover, Yishai offers no
further comments to explain his failure, for he still did not in-
tend to bring David forward. The only thing that he has to say at
this time is COME LET US DINE FOR THE SACRIFICE IS READY AND
THE TABLE IS SET. Scripture does not record this comment, for
there is no purpose in doing so. However, from Shmuel's reply
we can see that this must have been Yishai's response.

AND SHMUEL SAID: SEND FOR HIM AND BRING HIM, FOR WE SHALL NOT DINE UNTIL HE COMES HERE (ibid.). I have not come to your home to dine. I have come for one of your sons! Shmuel would not have refused to dine unless Yishai had first invited him to do so.

AND THEY SENT AND BROUGHT HIM. AND HE WAS RED-HEADED, WITH BEAUTIFUL EYES AND A PLEASANT APPEARANCE (ibid. :12). Scripture's description conceals more than it reveals. The only thing that we can infer is that David made less of an impression on the prophet than did Eliav — Yishai's first-born — who was tall and impressive looking. Before Shmuel stood a short red-head and the prophet was temporarily perplexed. Could this one succeed as king?

AND GOD SAID: ARISE AND ANOINT HIM, FOR THIS IS HE [WHO SHALL BE KING] ... AND HE ANOINTED HIM IN THE MIDST OF HIS BROTHERS (ibid. :13-14). All clearly saw that Shmuel acted as God's vehicle. Even Eliav — David's brother — saw this, but his attitude and the attitude of the other brothers toward David was no different as a result! The following quotations clearly indicate that nothing changed.

ONE PUZZLE AFTER ANOTHER

In the remaining verses of the chapter, as well as in the following chapter, the puzzle becomes even more complex.

From the time when he was anointed, the Divine spirit rested upon David and left Shaul — replaced by a spirit of melancholy which God sent upon him. Doeg the Edomite had keen perception and saw the change that had occurred in both David and Shaul. He decided to take advantage of the circumstances and began his diabolical plot against David. Through his counsel, David was hired as a musician, ostensibly to soothe Shaul's temper, but in reality to create a feeling of jealousy.

David became the king's most beloved helper and his personal attendant. Even so, he was not relieved of his responsibility of tending his father's flocks. Rather, he travelled back and forth between his duties in Shaul's court and his father's flocks in Beis Lechem. He was a shepherd before he was anointed and a shepherd he remained after being anointed. In the meantime, war approached.

The Phillistines gathered to wage war. In their arrogance, they pretended to be reluctant to spill blood and taunted Shaul and Israel: "If you are God's people, why should you have to wage war? Choose one from among you to do battle with Golias and God, your Lord, will deliver you from his hand!" [See 17:8-10]

Neither the spirit of Shaul nor that of his army was aroused by Golias' blasphemy. They were already incapable of waging war on their own and there was none among them valiant enough to take on Golias. Though many of Shaul's men would have been prepared to give their lives to save Israel, none saw themselves as being capable of doing battle with Golias. They could not depend upon a miracle, for perhaps they were not worthy of having a miracle performed in their merit and Divine anger would strike the community instead. Fearing and trembling, none of them knew from where their salvation would come.

However, there were eleven men there who did know what the source of their savation would be. Nine of them — Yishai, David and his seven brothers — had witnessed the prophet's action and knew who God's anointed was. Shmuel, God's seer who had anointed David. was also present. There was another person present, Doeg ha-Edomi. In his great wisdom, he knew who God's anointed one was, even though he had not been a witness. Of all of these, not one directed David to do battle and bring Israel her salvation. Why?

AND THE PHILLISTINE [GOLIAS] CAME FORWARD IN THE MORNING

AND IN THE EVENING FOR FORTY DAYS (ibid. :16). Twice daily Golias would declare: I HAVE BLASPHEMED THE HOST OF ISRAEL. GIVE ME A MAN AND WE SHALL DO BATTLE WITH EACH OTHER (ibid. :10).

Three of Yishai's sons accompanied Shaul to war. AND DAVID WAS THE YOUNGEST (ibid. :14) — he was not even considered worthy of serving among the multitudes. David was not considered fit for war, but was suited for an additional mission aside from his resposibilities toward Shaul and his father's flocks.

At his father's behest, David came to the encampment to inquire about his brothers' well-being. There he heard the blasphemies of the Phillistine — the son of his grandmother Ruth's sister. And there he volunteered to stand up to him and thereby remove Israel's shame.

The events that took place deserve close examination.

Together with all those who were gathered there, David heard the words of the Phillistine as well as Shaul's subsequent declaration. AND HE [SHAUL] SAID: MEN OF ISRAEL! HAVE YOU SEEN THIS MAN WHO COMES UP AGAINST US? HE COMES TO SHAME ISRAEL! AND IT SHALL BE THAT THE MAN WHO SHALL STRIKE HIM DOWN WILL BE REWARDED BY THE KING WITH GREAT WEALTH AND HE [THE KING] WILL GIVE HIM HIS DAUGHTER AND HIS [THE MAN WHO KILLS GOLIAS] FATHER'S HOUSE WILL BE MADE FREE IN ISRAEL (ibid. :25).

Why did David immediately ask the people in the encampment WHAT SHALL BE DONE FOR THE MAN WHO SHALL STRIKE DOWN THIS PHILLISTINE (ibid. :26), waiting for them to repeat the promises that Shaul had enunciated? Had he not heard the king's words as well as they had?

AND ELIAV, HIS OLDER BROTHER, HEARD HIM [DAVID] SPEAKING TO THE PEOPLE, AND ELIAV BECAME ANGRY WITH DAVID AND HE SAID: WHY DID YOU COME DOWN [TO THE ENCAMPMENT] AND WITH

WHOM HAVE YOU LEFT THE FEW SHEEP IN THE WILDERNESS. I AM
AWARE OF YOUR INIQUITY AND YOUR EVIL WAYS. YOU HAVE COME
DOWN TO SEE THE WAR (ibid. :28). Eliav spoke to him harshly de-
spite the fact that he knew that David was God's anointed. He
asks David why he has come down though he knew that it was
at their father's behest. He accuses him of abandoning the flock,
though Scripture tells us (ibid. :20) that David had left them in the
care of a watchman. He told David: "I am aware of your iniquity
and your evil ways." Is this how one speaks to God's anointed?
Furthermore, Shmuel had thought Eliav worthy of being
anointed, and would have done so had God not told him that
David was the one who was worthy. How could a person of
such stature say of David, "I am aware of your iniquity ..." What
did Eliav know?

AND DAVID SAID: WHAT HAVE I DONE NOW (ibid. :29). It would
seem that David is saying, "Generally, when you are angry with
me, your anger is not unfounded. But now, what have I done?"

AND HE [DAVID] TURNED AWAY FROM HIM AND FACED ANOTHER
AND ASKED AS HE HAD BEFORE. AND HE ANSWERED HIM AS HAD
THE FIRST (ibid. :30). David had heard Shaul's declaration himself.
He had already asked what would be done for the person who
struck down Golias and had received an answer. Why did he
pose the question again?

Know that when David stepped forward to do battle with Golias, he did not rely upon miraculous assistance. He knew that he
possessed sufficient strength and valor to stike down the Phillistine hero. He even had no need for a sword. A small stone
deftly aimed would be sufficient to lodge in the Phillistine
strongman's forehead, piercing the armor and skull as if they
were made of soft clay.

This confidence is apparent from the incident that David told
Shaul about the lion and the bear. Only one sheep had been tak-

en from his flock. Rather than being overjoyed that he had himself not been injured, David went to rescue the sheep from the lion. When the lion attacked him, he grabbed him by his mane and used him to kill the bear, killing both animals as one. No man would place himself in such danger to save one sheep unless he knew that he possessed superior strength. David had great strength and courage, yet Shaul tells him: YOU CAN NOT GO TO DO BATTLE WITH THIS PHILLISTINE, FOR YOU ARE BUT A YOUNG MAN (ibid. :33).

THIS WAS FROM GOD

All that we have seen regarding David until this point is a linked chain of events that the Creator wonderously formed so as to bring the light of *mashiach* to the world. In His profound wisdom, He saw fit to veil this light within a curtain of darkness that will only part when the time arrives for it to be revealed. The strength of the revealed light will be directly proportionate to the depth in which it was concealed.

Why was it necessary to conceal this light so deeply? It is the Divine will that when the light of *mashiach* appears, all darkness will be dispelled and all that had previously been hidden in the darkness will be revealed. Darkness will no longer be dark and the night shall be as light as day. Darkness and light will no longer exist as opposites, for both had been created from the primordial light and will return to their original state.

When God chooses to invest mortal man with His honor, to make him master over all of creation, to crown him with sovereignty that is an example of His own and to give him eternal dominion, He first makes him master over himself so that he might not become haughty. God places a guard over him to insure that he does not become subject to the evil designs of others nor to his own foibles. He who is perfect in three traits — seeing only good, who is humble and who has a generous soul

39

— is worthy of sovereignty. It was in this manner that God made David His anointed king and this will typify the *mashiach*, may he be revealed to us speedily and in our time.

See how many veils God employed to conceal the light of David before he was deemed worthy of sovereignty. The light which was seen in David was first revealed in our forefather, Avraham. It was concealed and revealed over and over again until David became king. But even in David, the light was not revealed in its full luminence, for the generation was not worthy. It will only shine forth with its maximum strength in *mashiach* at the end of time.

After Avraham, the light of *mashiach* was divided into two. Half was concealed in the earth, in the progeny of Amon and Moav. The other half remained revealed and was passed on to Yitzchok and through him to Yaakov. It was passed on to Yehudah and it was then that the light began to become luminous, for all saw that he was worthy of sovereignty. This light continued to shine, growing brighter as it passed on to Yehudah's son Peretz. It was concealed again during the years in Egypt, becoming luminous again in Nachshon ben Aminadav who was one of those who departed from Egypt. It then became concealed again during the time of Elimelech — Nachshon's son — of whom all had said: "This is the one whom we had hoped would sit on the throne of Israel. Behold he has fled to Moav!"

It was then that God chose to reveal the hidden light that had been concealed in the fields of Moav. It was His profound counsel to return Ruth to Beis Lechem, to rejoin the two halves of the light. Boaz, son of Salmon, son of Nachshon, was to bear a child through Ruth, daughter of Eglon, who returned from the fields of Moav to her roots — Avraham's credo of kindness.

A THIN LINE

When Boaz died immediately after marrying Ruth, darkness

once again fell upon the earth and the light of *mashiach* was once again concealed. Many thought that God was displeased that the progeny of Amon and Moav had become mixed within Israel. Ruth was at fault for Boaz's death and the child who would be the result of their union — if a child would be born — would be unfit.

The halachah which had distinguished between a Moabite [who was forbidden to be accepted as a convert] and a Moabitess [who could be accepted] was still tenuous and many found fault with the decision. Review *Megillas Ruth* and you will see that from the point where Ruth's pregnancy is mentioned until the end of the *megillah*, no mention is made of the Sages and others who were witness to the marriage of Boaz and Ruth. Even Ruth herself, Oved's mother, is no longer mentioned. Mention is made of the women and neighbors, who — in their compassion — referred to the child as "the son of Naomi". It is as if they were trying to conceal Ruth's role and thereby spared Naomi embarrassment, for she was partially responsible for all that had transpired.

The halachah permitting a Moabitess hung, as it were, on a thin line. No one was able to declare with certainty that it was correct. God alone knew that the halachah was valid and that all that took place between Boaz and Ruth was for the sake of heaven so that the light of *mashiach* might be revealed.

Oved — Ruth's son — became an adult. All saw that he was good and pious. Their fears were allayed and they said: "Had he, God forbid, been unfit, it is impossible that he be so pious and righteous."

This reaction was further strengthened after Yishai was born, for all saw that he was completely pure, lacking any trace of sin. They then said: "The spirit of God guided Boaz and the Sages when they ruled that Ruth might enter the assembly of God. They acted in accordance with the Torah."

Yishai bore six sons, each and everyone of them like refined flour. In all of Beis Lechem there were none as righteous. Valiant and strong in Torah, they enjoyed the full measure of all that is good in this world. There was now a three-ply cord — Oved, Yishai and Eliav [Yishai's first-born] — and it could not be torn. All those who had previously had doubts, who had said to themselves: "One should never think that punishment will not come [even if it does not do so immediately]" were now relieved. Three generations had been born of the union and all were righteous. There was now no reason to fear punishment [for having allowed Ruth to convert]. All saw that Yishai's house was refined and pure. There was no blemish to be found in his family. The light for which all hoped and prayed was destined to be issued by his descendents.

And then David was born and a dark cloud filled the sky in a manner that had never before been seen. Again, no one — save God himself — knew where the light was concealed. This veil — the last before the great revelation — was the thickest of all. God took the light of *mashiach* and concealed it from everyone. The light was now hidden in darkness.

There are children whose talents are concealed from outsiders but whose parents are aware of their abilities. Then there are children whose talents are obvious to outsiders but remain concealed from their parents. There are even some whose talents are hidden from everyone, but surely they can not be concealed from the greatest prophet of the generation — a man to whom God granted wisdom and the ability to see from one side of the world to the other.

David's secret was concealed from his father and mother, from all of the people who lived in his time and even from Shemuel, the prophet who did not recognize David's abilities even after he first saw him, until God told him (*Shmuel* I 16:13): ARISE AND ANOINT HIM KING, FOR IT IS HE.

GOD SAID TO DWELL IN DARKNESS

Our Sages taught: Because of Yishai's great trepidation of being guilty of even the slightest sin, he became fearful in his old age and said: "Perhaps my grandfather Boaz and his court ruled erroneously and I am unfit to be a part of the assembly of God. How can I live with a pure Israelite woman when I may well be a Moabite?"

Yishai already had six sons and two daughters when this doubt arose in his mind. How was he to rectify the past? The traits of the wicked are far different than those of the righteous. The wicked have no fear of sin. And even if they do fear, they are afraid only of punishment. When they see that they have mired themselves excessively in transgression, they abandon hope of escaping punishment and continue to sin.

But the righteous do not act in this manner. Their major fear is sin itself — not its punishment. Therefore, even when they see that they have transgressed and will not be able to escape punishment, they still do not abandon themselves to even the slightest sin.

Because of his fears that he might be unfit, Yishai left his wife for a number of years and his sons knew why he had done so.

However, Yishai was a righteous man and said to himself: "God did not create the world to leave it unpopulated but rather to be settled. It is not right for a man to live without a woman." What did he do? Some years after having separated himself from his wife, he took one of the gentile maidservants in his house and said to her: "I am liberating you conditionally. If I am fit to be accepted into the assembly of God, then your liberation is valid and you shall be my wife in accordance with the laws of Moshe and Israel. But, if I am unfit, then your liberation is cancelled and you remain a maidservant and are thus permitted to a Moabite as well."

Yishai's wife was exceedingly righteous. Her husband's separation distressed her greatly, for she wanted to bear more of his children. When the maidservant noticed her distress, she said: "Do with me that which Leah did with her sister Rachel." Thus, Yishai's wife took the maidservant's place and sanctified herself, praying to God that He grant her another child. It was God's design that Yishai remain unaware that his wife had switched places with the maidservant. Three months later, his sons noiced that their mother was pregnant and told their father: "Our mother has become pregnant through infidelity. She should be killed as should the child that she carries."

At this point Yishai was greatly troubled and it was as if his heart had stopped beating. He told his sons: "Allow her to give birth and do not give cause for slander to be levied against you. The child that will be born shall be abhorred and will be your servant." Yishai thought to prevent the child — David — from being accepted into the community of Israel in this manner without having to publicize the fact that he was a *mamzer*.

Thus, we find that David said of himself (*Tehillim* 69:9): I WAS STRANGE TO MY BROTHERS — for they considered me to be illegitimate. AN ALIEN TO THE CHILDREN OF MY MOTHER — for they suspected her of infidelity.

SUFFERING BORNE WITH JOY AND LOVE

Mental anguish is painful. Not every person has the ability to accept this kind of suffering with love. In some, it can bring them to strike out against God and question His motives, as it were. Sometimes, suffering can lead a person to an even worse end; because they are persecuted and isolated, they are led to abandon God completely and completely forsake the source of life itself. In such cases, pain become the root cause for denial of God. This is what happens to weak people who are unable to bear their suffering.

David, however, was the most valiant man who ever lived. What was his strength? He was able to withstand personal suffering better than anyone else. It was for this reason that God placed him at the midpoint of history, so that he would be able to bear all the generations that preceded him and followed him — just as the center beam bears the weight of the entire roof.

The sons of the tribe of Yehudah matured early and while still young, already possessed full strength and wisdom. This can be seen from Yehudah himself. In but twenty-two years, three generations emerged from Yehudah: his sons Er, Onan and Shelah from his first wife, Peretz and Zerach from his union with Tamar, as well as Chetzron and Chamul — Peretz's sons. We find a similar phenomenon in the descendents of Calev son of Yefuneh: Chur [Calev's son], Uri [his grandson] and Betzalel [his great-grandson]. When Betzalel was but thirteen years old, God filled him with wisdom, foresight and knowledge giving him the ability to build the Tabernacle of God in accordance with God's design.

Likewise, the sons of the tribe of Yehudah were not subject to the ravages of aging as were other people and they remained as strong as lions until their dying days. These qualities were surely true of David, for he was the essence of the tribe and its most select member.

While David was still a child, he was already aware of his destiny. While yet in the crib, his mother would whisper to him: "You are pure my son — sanctified from the womb — as is your mother. Do not allow your mood to falter because of the suffering that you shall endure. Accept it with love and with trust in God ... you will not be [eternally] humiliated." All this David heard and understood.

When he grew up and saw the fences which separated him from his brothers, he understood and accepted them.

Our Sages taught: Yishai was the greatest man of his generation. Wherever he went, masses of Jews would come to greet him and would accompany him when he departed. His seven sons followed in his footsteps and were all considered to be distinguished. They too would accompany him on his travels and the honor paid Yishai was theirs as well. Only the young David did not keep their company. They drove him away and held him in contempt — but David did not depart and returned their hatred with love, for he knew that they acted for the sake of heaven. He would justify their attitude by telling himself: "It is not me that they hate, but rather it is sin. I detest sin no less than they."

When the people saw that David's brothers kept him at a distance, they said: "There must be reason for them doing so, there must be something evil in the home of Yishai."

Because none of the people knew the real reason why Yishai's sons kept their distance from David, they began to imagine all kinds of things that were not true of David and heaped accusations upon him. At first they did so with doubt as to whether he was really guilty. But when no one come forward to deny them, the doubtful accusations in time were accepted as being truthful and everyone in Israel "knew" that David was "evil". There was no one who hesitated in wounding David's pride, for they all said: "By humiliating David we give honor to the House of Yishai. If those who know him well detest him, then we should surely do so."

Sent away from his own home, a pariah in the community at large, David found rich pasture and clear, flowing water for his soul's hunger for God in the wilderness to which he fled. There — apart from society —where no one would know or see, he sought to draw close to God.

How numerous are the distractions and stumbling blocks in the way of a person who seeks pleasure in cleaving to God when he is in the company of his fellow man! Distractions stand in one's way and the eyes of others watching are damaging to he who seeks to draw close to God. Man is constantly distracted — either by the love of those who are fond of him or by the enmity of those who hate him. When does he have the time to study the statutes of God and know His laws so that he might cleave to Him?

David, however, spent all of his days in the wilderness, free from the love of his fellow man and their longing for him and free from their enmity. Without the distractions they bring and the eyes with which they observe, he was able to devote his body and soul to God alone. God was both his father and his brother. All of the pleasures with which society occupies itself were meaningless to him. How could they be compared to the joy which David found in basking in the light of the *Shechinah*, in His goodness and kindness in the wilderness where no stranger would interfere and no eye would see him. He therefore declared (*Tehillim* 119:71): IT WAS GOOD THAT I WAS AFFLICTED [when I lived with others] SO THAT I MIGHT LEARN YOUR STATUTES [in the wilderness]. David found joy in the suffering caused him by others, for without them he would have never been able to achieve such great cleaving to the living God.

How beautiful is the wilderness. The skies and clouds above, every grain of sand below, the thorns and the thistles — they all joined David in his songs of praise to God. There was no other sound there that might interfere with his song. How pleasant are the crevices and caves of the wilderness. When man enters them he is alone in the universe and all that one can see is the radiance of the *Shechinah*.

How sweet is the thirst one experiences in the wilderness if it is transformed into a thirst for God. The soul thirsts for God and the flesh pines for Him [see *Tehillim* 63:2]. David was unwilling to leave until his soul is sated by the milk and bread of his prayers, for God's kindness is greater than life itself!

47

How joyous is the darkness of the wilderness and the chill of the nights, for it is then that God reveals Himself to David and the night becomes light for him.

David therefore declares: YOU HAVE DONE GOOD FOR YOUR SER-VANT [and if I should forget and ask You for another kind of good, do not listen to me]. GOD, MAY IT BE AS YOU HAVE DECREED [i.e., do unto me as You have decreed and not as I desire] (ibid. 119:65).

WITH BEAUTIFUL EYES AND A PLEASANT APPEARANCE

At times David returned to visit his father's home. He makes his appearance in Beis Lechem and the people looked at him askance. He had not spent his time eating until sated or engaging in bodily pleasures. He was not clothed in beautiful garments. When a feeling of jealousy passed through his heart, he wept and fasted, donned sackcloth and concentrated his entire soul in prayer to God that his thoughts not be considered sinful. How could those who saw him appreciate his beauty? He was burned by the fierce sun of the desert, his eyes shone with the intensity of one who cleaves to God. His flesh was drawn, he was shorter than the other members of his family and his clothing was tattered. All who saw him wondered: "Where have you been David? What have you been doing?"

If, by chance, a thief quietly entered the city and escaped without being caught, people would immediately say: "David, where were you last night. Bring witnesses to corroborate your alibi." Could David tell them: "I was seeking God's kindness. I was singing God's praises." Even when David knew who had committed the crime, his lips were sealed. In his mind, it was preferable to subject himself to shame and castigation rather than to use the Torah as a vehicle for proving his innocence. For the sake of God's name he was prepared to bear denigration, so that God's name might later be sanctified when the generation would recognize that all that had transpired was God's design.

"I shall return the stolen property," David would answer.

"You are the shame of our nation," the residents of Beis Lechem would castigate.

"You are a stigma to your father's house," his brothers would add.

When the people saw David's reactions and his ability never to be caught in the act, they once again decided that the root of his "evil" must be the source from which he stemmed. Was David not a direct descendent of Ruth the Moabite? Whatever level of piety that Boaz possessed must have found expression in Yishai and his seven other sons. All of the refuse which came along with Ruth had found expression in David alone. The old thoughts once again came to fore and were the subject of everyone's discussions — from the members of the *sanhedrin* who sat in judgement at the gates of the city and deliberated once again about the earlier ruling until the drunkards who sat in the beer halls who composed songs that ridiculed David.

Why was David subject to such humiliation? The time had not yet come for his true character to be revealed. David had not yet consumed the full measure of the cup of denigration which he had to drink on behalf of the world that he was destined to lead.

Until that time came, David was prepared to joyously accept every travail and every anxiety which was his lot, never asking God to spare him from his trials. David had "beautiful eyes" — he saw all that was happening to him through rose-colored glasses. He was of "pleasant appearance" — everything that he looked at was pleasant in his eyes and he therefore sought no other good.

When did David come to possess "beautiful eyes" and a "good appearance" in the eyes of others as well? Only when he was anointed as king and the time had arrived for him to be revealed. Before that time, he could see but his true character was invisible. He viewed everything as "pleasant" but was not viewed as being "pleasant" himself.

His brothers and the members of his father's household knew no respite when David was in their midst, so they sent him off to tend their father's flocks in the wilderness. It was only then that they knew peace, as did David himself. From then on he spent most of his time alone and his visits home were infrequent.

YISHAI'S EIGHTH SON

The House of Yishai had despaired of having God's glory emanate from within it because of the shame caused by David. It was God's will to conceal His plan from His loved ones until the appropriate time arrived. Shmuel came with a horn of anointing oil as a messenger of God to anoint a king from the House of Yishai. Aside from the "source of shame" that was a part of the house, all of them were worthy of becoming king. Yishai brought all of his seven sons forward so that God might indicate which one of them was most fit in His eyes. However, Yishai did not call David to come forward, for God has not as yet indicated to either Yishai or to Shmuel who David was and what he was destined to become. Until that point, Yishai had seven sons. It was as if God had now given him an eighth son — the most honored of his children — David.

ARE THERE NO MORE YOUTHS (Shmuel I 16:11)? God placed the words in the mouth of His prophet. Had Shmuel asked, "Are there no more sons?", Yishai would have answered erroneously that there were no more, for he did not consider David to be his son. The righteous Yishai would have inadvertently lied. But the term YOUTHS is all inclusive — implying servants and other members of the household, a criteria that David met.

AND HE [YISHAI] REPLIED: THERE IS A LITTLE ONE REMAINING AND

HE IS TENDING THE FLOCKS (ibid. :11). Yishai responded to Shmuel rhetorically, asking the prophet not to remind him of the sin that had brought on so much anguish. "Allow him [David] to continue to tend the flocks. It is better for us and for him! God will guide as to what we should do."

Shmuel replied: SEND FOR HIM AND BRING HIM (ibid.).

The truly righteous do not attempt to probe that which is beyond them. Once Shmuel told Yishai to bring David, he questioned no further, for one may not try to "outsmart" a prophet.

AND THEY SENT AND BROUGHT HIM. AND HE WAS RED-HEADED, WITH BEAUTIFUL EYES AND A PLEASANT APPEARANCE (ibid. :12). Was this one fit to be king? AND GOD SAID, ARISE AND ANOINT HIM FOR THIS IS HE [WHO SHALL BE KING]. AND HE ANOINTED HIM IN THE MIDST OF HIS BROTHERS (ibid. :13-14).

All of a sudden, Yishai understood all that had happened from the time that David was conceived until now. He understood that an eighth son had now been born to him. The efforts that David and his mother had made to conceal their righteousness made them all the more precious in Yishai's eyes. Now that he comprehended, he began to refer to him as "my son."

Eliav, who witnessed the entire episode, did not understand the mysterious ways of God. In his eyes the matter was beyond comprehension. "There is one of my mother's sons who is unfit. Is he to be king?"

This is the way the righteous act. When Divine secrets are revealed to them, they do not convey them to others, but wait for God to make the matter common knowledge. Yishai who merited understanding, now knew that David was fit. Eliav's time had not yet come and he therefore had to continue to wait.

David's measure of anguish had not yet been filled. More valiant than all others, more righteous, wiser — now that he was

51

about to be king, it was fitting that he also be more humble. He was to continue to suffer anguish and to be persecuted — even though he had already been anointed — until the crown of sovereignty was actually placed upon his head.

Even his father Yishai — who was now aware of his true stature — was not permitted to hasten the end of David's suffering. Let the world continue in its manner and God would do as He saw fit. All that had transpired until now was the will of God and He had not involved any man in His design. God would bring matters to their fruition. In the meantime David would return to tend the flocks while his three brothers joined Shaul in battle.

ELIAV'S INNER STRUGGLE

AND HE ANOINTED HIM IN THE MIDST OF HIS BROTHERS (ibid.). Why did Eliav see fit to continue to drive David away? Did he not know that God had anointed him as king of the nation? Eliav's behavior can be compared to that of the "generation of wisdom" — the wise man and members of the *sanhedrin* who joined Korach in disputing Moshe's leadership. Can one contend that the beginning of their dispute was not for the sake of Heaven? The Torah (*Bemidbar* 16:2) speaks of them in glowing terms, referring to them as PRINCES OF THE CONGREGATION, THE ELECT OF THE ASSEMBLY, MEN OF REKNOWN. It is clear that they were righteous, wise and pure of heart. They knew that God had spoken to Moshe directly, they saw that he was the instrument through which God had performed His wonders and miracles, yet they did not hesitate to contest his leadership!

The later commentators offer the following explanation to resolve this question. The people indeed recognized Moshe's greatness and knew that there had never been one like him who had seen God "face to face". At the same time, they also saw a number of things in Moshe that they could not understand and that were, in their opinion, intolerable. In their view, the verse YOU SHALL NOT FEAR ANY MAN (*Devarim* 1:17) applied to everyone — even to Moshe — and they thus did not hesitate. At first they thought that they must be mistaken, suspecting themselves of ulterior motives or of self-interest. But when they examined themselves thoroughly and saw that their motives were pure and devoid of any trace of seeking personal prestige, they asked themselves: "How is it possible that we should dispute Moshe and find fault with his behavior? It is obvious that in the end, Moshe is truthful as are all his actions. Why have we been prevented from seeing this?"

Nevertheless, they disputed Moshe's leadership saying: "If our contentions are shown to be true, then we have been zealous for the sake of Heaven. And if in the end Moshe is vindicated and we are found to be culpable for having disputed his leadership, what difference does it make? Who are we and what value is their to our lives if we substitute darkness for light and fail to pursue truth!? No matter what happens we shall lose nothing and the name of Heaven will be sanctified through our actions."

We see how committed they were to truth. Why then were they punished? Because they should not have persisted in the dispute when they saw that Moshe was vindicated. There is no wisdom, nor counsel nor understanding in the face of God's design. When they were specifically warned to cease the dispute, they should have accepted the command. Because they failed to do so, they were punished.

Eliav's conduct can be understood in the same light. In his heart Eliav knew that he was acting for Heaven's sake and that there was no self-interest that would make him culpable. He "knew" what David was — a stranger and no son of Yishai. He saw God's actions as evidenced through His prophet. How was he to resolve the seeming contradictions. Was it permissible for one to subjugate the truth that he perceived when no Divine warning had been forthcoming?

Nevertheless, Eliav did not persist in contesting the choice of David. When he saw that David was the instrument of God's salvation, he humbled himself before David. What Yishai had understood earlier, Eliav now comprehended. David was pure, a genuine brother of his. Moreover, through the anguish that he had suffered, he had been refined and was more worthy of sovereignty than Eliav.

SERVANT OF GOD

I AM YOUR SERVANT, THE SON OF YOUR MAIDSERVANT (Tehillim 116:16). Our Sages (Yalkut Shimoni) explained: One can not compare the fealty of a servant born into servitude with that of one who is himself sold into servitude.

A true servant has no desires of his own. His greatest pleasure is when his king shows him his love by inviting him into the innermost chambers alone, enjoying his songs and music. And if the king should choose to send his servant on a mission to a distant land, he willingly and lovingly accepts the mission even though doing so causes him to be separated from his king, for he has no desire other than that of his master.

Thus, David accepted the crown of sovereignty that had been placed upon his head, for it was God's will that this be done. David himself sought only to be close to God — in the wilderness or within the community, in the sheep pens or in the chambers of the palace. Indeed, what use did he have for the trappings of royalty when he felt closer to God when alone in the wilderness? He accepted sovereignty because such was the will of God. But he made no attempts to bring it to fruition more quickly.

God who sent His prophet to anoint him would decide when the proper time had come to fulfill that will.

AS YISHAI HAD COMMANDED HIM

David did not join the battle with the Phillistines because of the motives that Eliav perceived — YOU HAVE COME DOWN TO SEE THE WAR (*Shmuel I* 17:28). God had not yet ordered David to take up his role; he came to the encampment because his father had instructed him to do so. AND DAVID AROSE IN THE MORNING (ibid. :20) — the righteous undertake their missions in the morning [i.e., without delay]. AND HE LEFT THE SHEEP WITH A WATCHMAN (ibid.) — in refutation of Eliav's remonstration that he had ABANDONED THE FEW SHEEP (ibid.). AND HE CARRIED (ibid.) — on his shoulders a heavy burden of provisions for his three brothers and for the officer. AND HE TRAVELLED (ibid.) — a great distance, from Beis Lechem to the encampment which was between Socho and Azeka. AS YISHAI HAD COMMANDED HIM (ibid.) — and not because of his own will.

REVEALING A LITTLE AND CONCEALING A GREAT DEAL

When David entered the encampment and heard the blasphemies of Golias, he knew that he had the ability to strike down the Phillistine, just as he had struck down the lions and bears earlier, without endangering himself and without necessitating a miracle. No one else was aware of David's physical prowess, for it was concealed as were all of his other powers.

Were he not of heroic strength he would not have accepted Golias' challenge. He would not have relied upon God's coming to assist His anointed one, for the time had not yet come for him to be revealed. He had no right to hurry the fruition of the Divine plan.

And even when he entered the fray, relying upon his own prowess rather than upon miraculous intervention, he remained reluctant to publicize his abilities. He had no desire that it be said, "David is a hero. He has endangered himself so as to bring Israel salvation and is therefore worthy of praise." He strived to conceal the signficance of that which he was about to do.

David heard the proclamation read in the encampment: "Men of Israel. Have you seen the man who arises against us? He who strikes him down shall be enriched by the king and will be given the king's daughter as a reward." David utilized the proclamation as a means of further concealing his powers. He turned to those around him and asked: "What shall be done for the man who strikes down the Phillistine?" The answer is given him but he continues to ask. David understood that by asking the question again and again, those around him would say to themselves: "Look at this unknown young shepherd! He fancies the king's daughter!" His repeated questioning would make him look foolish. He was about to accomplish a great deed and his reward would be humiliation rather than honor! This is the character of David — king of Israel and the anointed of God for all generations.

Even when he spoke to Shaul before going out to battle Golias, David was coy and revealed only a bit of his strength while concealing the zeal for God's honor that burned within him because of the Phillistine's blasphemy. He hid his desire to avenge God's honor behind a mask of humility and prayer, telling Shaul: GOD, WHO SAVED ME FROM THE LION AND FROM THE BEAR, HE WILL SAVE ME FROM THIS PHILLISTINE (ibid. :37). This too was part of David's effort to conceal his true motivation, as can be seen from the words of the people who brought him to Shaul, saying: "This is the man who desires your daughter and for her sake he will slay the Phillistine."

David was dressed in Shaul's armaments [see :40] but removed them so that the people not pay him too much attention. Everything that David did represented a conscious and concentrated effort to conceal his greatness and stress his worthlessness.

THE VOICE OF GOD'S ANOINTED SPEAKS

But David's efforts to mask his true identity were of no avail when he approached Golias and spoke in front of his own people and the Phillistines. It was no longer David who spoke nor did he express his own thoughts. The spirit of God had entered him and spoke from within him. The time for the revealing of the true David had arrived.

The Phillistine had crushed the spirit of David's people, casting fear and dread. There was no one who had the ability to answer the Phillistine in an appropriate fashion. Now, all of the eyes of Israel were focused on the middle ground between the two warriors. It was no longer young David who stood ready to do battle with the blaspheming Golias. It was Israel's sword and pride, the sword that was to bring vengeance to the Eternal Covenant that was raised against the Phillistine. And the sword had two edges: one to reply to the blasphemer and one to slay him.

Now all would hear the difference between Golias, the son of Orpah who had chosen to return to the fields of Moav, and between the descendent of Ruth who had gone to Beis Lechem.

AND THE PHILLISTINE SAID TO DAVID: AM I A DOG THAT YOU COME AGAINST ME WITH STICKS? (ibid. :43). When Golias saw David approaching, his arrogance disappeared and he no longer blasphemed. He had but one query, which God phrased for him in a way that answered his own question. All that Golias was concerned with was the affront to his honor. He no longer remembered that he was there to do battle for his nation. His sense of security was gone, he was enraged and therefore cursed David using the name of his god. And David replied: "Your god has a mouth but does not speak! The one who curses in his name will end up the same." The Phillistine, in his great anger, was silenced.

But the full measure of the Phillistine's shame, which would culminate with his death, had not yet been revealed. He was therefore led to speak again.

AND THE PHILLISTINE SAID TO DAVID: COME TO ME (ibid. :44). Of course David would come to him, for that was God's design. AND I WILL SERVE YOUR FLESH TO THE BIRDS AND TO THE ANIMALS (ibid.). In reply, David taunted Golias. "Have you lost your mind!? Have you ever seen a domesticated animal eat human flesh!? Similarly, I have no fear that you will serve my flesh to the birds. Moreover, you used a future form [WILL SERVE]. Of what happened in the past you have no knowledge. How can you know what will happen in the future. Be silent Phillistine, for you have sealed your own judgement."

AND DAVID SAID TO THE PHILLISTINE: YOU APPROACH ME WITH A SWORD, AND WITH A SPEAR (ibid. :45) — but our God disables warriors, snapping their bows and breaking their spears. AND I COME IN THE NAME OF THE GOD OF HOSTS, THE GOD OF THE BATTLES OF ISRAEL WHOM YOU HAVE BLASPHEMED (ibid.) — to restore honor to the God who is glorious, the living and eternal God. ON THIS DAY (ibid. :46) — just as this day is clear, so too is your fate clear. GOD WILL DELIVER YOU TO MY HANDS (ibid.) — so do I ordain, and God will not refuse me for He is trusted to fulfill. AND I SHALL STRIKE YOU, AND I SHALL CUT OFF YOUR HEAD, AND I WILL MAKE THE CAMP OF THE PHILLISTINES CARCASSES THIS DAY FOR THE BIRDS AND FOR THE ANIMALS AND ALL OF THE WORLD SHALL KNOW THAT ISRAEL HAS A GOD (ibid.).

The words are not David's but the Holy Spirit which spoke through him. And the word of God is action.

MAN HAS MANY THOUGHTS

At first David said to himself: "I will finish what I must do with the Phillistine and then I shall return to tend my father's flocks in the wilderness." But God had other designs and did not allow David to return. He took David from the flocks of sheep and brought him to shepherd the children of Israel. The time had come for David to ascend the throne.

David then thought: "The crown of God has been placed on my head. Let the honor of God's anointed spread among the people. They will see my glory and I shall transfer that glory to God, for alone I can not pay Him respect for I am nothing." But God had not as yet so commanded.

Even when David ascended the throne, his enemies were still more numerous than the hairs on his head. Everyone still recalled the humiliation that he had suffered at home, they had not forgotten the accusations — the thefts that he had not committed but had nevertheless returned. All who saw him ridiculed him. When God showered His bounty upon the people, it was in their merit. And when He brought them travail, David's sins were the cause. When the son of a Moabite becomes king, he can not expect his salvation to come from God!

Your time to reign had arrived David, but the time had not yet come for Israel to have you as king. Stiffen your resolve to suffer yet more on behalf of your nation. Pour out your feelings before your King and let your songs become your eternity and that of your people as well. The cup of your anguish is not yet full. You still have not found the second dove that your father Avraham lost and which was hidden in Amon.

Na'amah of Amon — she too is a necessary element for your sovereignty, like your mother Ruth. In the days of your son Shlomo she will be found and the cup will then be filled. Let Ruth the Moabite — your great-grandmother — dwell in your

59

house and remain alive until the era of your son Shlomo. To some she will be a source of pride, to others a reminder of sin, until Na'amah of Amon will come to the household of Shlomo.

Even then the measure of suffering that marks your reign shall not be filled. There are yet many battles awaiting you and your progeny against those who stand against God and His anointed. God alone is a "man of war" [see *Shemos* 15:3]. It is not fitting for man to engage in battle nor is that his true glory. The entire world suffers as a result of war — can man sit back and bask in glory? Make yourself a partner to the world's suffering until the time when anguish shall pass from the world. Then your serenity shall be returned and you will be compensated for your anguish. Then the greatness of your honor shall be revealed before all; in the days of a son of your son this shall come about, in the time of *mashiach*, speedily and in our time.

SHAVUOS — DAVID'S DAY

The festival of Shavuos is the *yahrtzeit* [anniversary of the death] of David. It is therefore customary in the Diaspora to gather in the synagogue on the second day of Shavuos, the day when David passed away. The entire Book of Psalms is publicly read and many candles are lit. In some communities it is customary to light one hundred and fifty candles corrssponding to the number of chapters in *Tehillim*. In Jerualem it is customary to visit the traditional site of David's grave so as to recall David's merit and his acts of righteousness on behalf of Israel.

Torah and Masorah

CHAPTER TWO

TORAH AND MASORAH

The Torah which we possess, all of its letters — including those written in either an enlarged or smaller size — and even all of the crowns placed upon various letters, is the very same Torah that God showed Moshe in the form of a black fire atop a white fire. It was this Torah that Moshe copied onto parchment. When Moshe transcribed from the script that he had seen, he also heard God dictate all of the words that he was writing. By hearing the words he was made aware of the *k'ri* [the manner in which the words are to be read] and by seeing the words he was made aware of the *k'siv* [the manner in which the words are to be spelled].

The Torah transcribed by Moshe was the first *sefer* Torah, regarding which the verse (*Devarim* 31:25-26) states: AND MOSHE COMMANDED THE LEVITES WHO CARRIED THE ARK OF THE COVENANT OF GOD SAYING: TAKE THIS SEFER TORAH AND PLACE IT BESIDE THE ARK OF THE COVENANT OF YOUR GOD AND IT SHALL BE THERE FOR YOU TO BEAR WITNESS. Later, Moshe wrote another twelve *sifrei* Torah and gave one to each of the tribes. He taught the people orally that which he himself had been taught by God — the general and specific principles, the derivations and allusions and all of the matters which are hidden within the text, within the letters, within their combinations, within the chapter divisions and within the volumes. To the extent that the generation was capable of absorbing, Moshe taught and brought them to understand at the time that he gave them the Torah scrolls that he had transcribed.

Using these scrolls, the scribes in the generations following Moshe transcribed additional *sifrei* Torah with caution and trepidation lest they err and alter even a single crown of a single letter. In subsequent generations other scribes copied the scrolls written by the first scribes. As additional copies were made, errors were sometimes made and the scrolls were therefore compared to the earlier scrolls which had been examined. Corrections were made accordingly.

As the generations passed, troubles increased. The *aron* containing the Torah written by Moshe was hidden and the first scrolls disappeared. At the same time, numerous additional copies were made. To ascertain that they were correct, they were compared to earlier scrolls that were still to be found and that had been examined and found to be correct. If minor differences were found between earlier versions of Torah scrolls, the Sages would establish the text based on that found in the majority of earlier scrolls. The Talmud (*Soferim* 6:4) records that three Torah scrolls were found in the courtyard of the *Beis ha-Mikdash*. In each there was a minor textual variation in one scroll that did not appear in the others. The Sages determined that the correct text was that which was to be found in two of the scrolls. They were thus able to once again establish a standard text to which all subsequent scrolls could be compared. In later generations, this practice was repeated so that we know that the text of the Torah that we have today is precisely the same as that written in Moshe's scroll according to God's dictation.

THE FIRST TORAH SCROLL

There is a difference of opinion among the Sages (*Gittin* 60a) regarding the first Torah scroll written by Moshe. R. Yochanan maintains that it was recorded in separate scrolls which were combined at the end of the forty years in the desert. Thus, all of

Bereishis was written at Mt. Sinai at the time that the Torah was received as was *Shemos* until *parashas Yisro*. As events occurred and as precepts were given, they were recorded in separate scrolls. At the end of the fortieth year, *Devarim* was written and then all of the scrolls were combined.

Reish Lakish maintains that the entire Torah was written at one time at the end of the forty years.

There is another dispute among the Sages (*Bava Basra* 15a) regarding the authorship of the last eight verses in *Devarim* which record the death of Moshe.

> *The verse (Devarim 34:5) states: AND MOSHE THE SERVANT OF GOD DIED THERE. Is it possible that Moshe was alive yet wrote AND MOSHE DIED THERE? Rather, until these verses Moshe wrote the text. From this verse on, the text was written by Yehoshua. This is the opinion of R. Yehudah and some say that it is the opinion of R. Nechemyah. R. Shimon said to him: Is it possible that the Torah [written by Moshe] was missing a single letter? The verse (ibid. 31:26) states: TAKE THIS SEFER TORAH AND PLACE IT BESIDE THE ARK OF THE COVENANT [and if the Torah was only completed by Yehoshua after Moshe's death, how could Moshe have referred to it as a sefer Torah]? Rather, until this point [i.e., the final eight verses] God dictated and Moshe wrote. From this point, God dictated and Moshe wrote with tears.*

The Vilna Gaon offers an interesting explanation as to the meaning of "and Moshe wrote with tears". The Hebrew word for tears — *dema* — is etymologically similar to the word *dimu'a* — mixed [see, for example, *Mishnah Terumah* 5:5]. When Moshe wrote the final eight verses, the letters were not separated into words but were mixed together so that different words could be read. Thus, the specific phrase AND MOSHE DIED THERE was not explicitly transcribed by Moshe even though the letters that form these words were written by him.

The letters of the Torah can be explained in additional ways, aside from the traditional combination of letters which has been passed down to us, depending on how they are combined. Our traditional combination of letters gives us the literal meaning of the Torah whereas other combinations offer mystical meanings. In these last eight verses of the Torah, Moshe was made aware of the mystical interpretation. The literal meaning of the words — which is obvious to us — remained concealed from him as he transcribed them.

GOD DICTATED AND MOSHE TRANSCRIBED

Although the entire Torah was given through Moshe, and indeed many of the sections begin with God speaking to Moshe, we find that when Moshe transcribed the text, he did not write AND GOD SPOKE TO ME, but AND GOD SPOKE TO MOSHE. Even in *Devarim*, where it seems that Moshe writes in first person [e.g., AND I PLEADED TO GOD (3:23), AND GOD SAID TO ME (ibid. :26)] or where he seems to be speaking for himself and for the entire community [e.g., AND WE TURNED AND WE WENT (ibid. 2:8)], the text is not Moshe's own narrative but the dictation of God.

In the introduction to his commentary to the Torah, Ramban notes the use of first person in *Devarim* in contrast to the other Books of the Torah. He writes:

It would seem that at the beginning of Bereishis the Torah should have said AND GOD SPOKE TO MOSHE, SAYING ALL OF THESE THINGS. However, there was a reason to begin the text without this type of preface, for Moshe did not transcribe the Torah as if he was speaking of himself in the way that we find with the Prophets who mention themselves. For example, we see that both Yechezkel (3:15) and Yirmiyahu (1:4) write: AND THE WORD OF GOD WAS ADDRESSED TO

ME. Moshe, on the other hand, wrote the history of the first generations, his own geneology and history in third person. [Even when recording speech directed to Moshe] the Torah (Shemos 6:2) states: AND GOD SPOKE TO MOSHE AND SAID TO HIM, as if Moshe was recounting a conversation between others. For this reason, Moshe is not mentioned in the Torah prior to his birth, as if someone else were telling the story.

And do not find difficulty in the fact that in Mishnah Torah [the Book of Devarim] Moshe does speak of himself — AND I PLEADED TO GOD (op. cit.)., for the beginning of Devarim begins with the preface THESE ARE THE WORDS THAT MOSHE SPOKE TO ALL OF ISRAEL and it is therefore as if he is quoting someone else. The reason why the Torah is written in this fashion [in contradistinction to the Prophets where first person is used] is because the Torah predates creation [see Shabbos 88b], not to speak of [predating] the birth of Moshe. As our tradition records (Devarim Rabbah 3), it was written as a black fire atop a white fire. Moshe was like a scribe copying from an older text and he therefore does not speak of himself. But it is true and clear that the entire Torah — from Bereishis to the last verse — was said by God to Moshe.

THE ORAL PART OF THE WRITTEN TORAH

Just as the explanation of the verses, the halachos which are derived from them and the orally transmitted Torah were all given to Moshe along with the written Torah, so too the written Torah itself — once it was given to Moshe — also included many orally transmitted instructions that pertain to the text. Moshe was not commanded to copy the text as he saw it — a black fire atop a white fire. Rather, he was told to transcribe it in a somewhat different form. At times, he made changes in the text itself [according to God's instructions] so that his transcription would be more understandable to those who would later study the Torah.

Ramban, in his introduction, writes:

We have another authentic tradition that the entire Torah consists of God's names — i.e., the letters can be divided into different word combinations [than the combinations we use to give us the words that we can understand]. For example, the words bereishis bara (Bereishis 1:1) could be divided as bereish yisbara. This is true of the entire Torah. Rabbeinu Shlomo [Rashi] shows in his commentary to the Talmud (Sukkah 45a, s.v. ani veho) how the Divine name of seventy-two letters can be found in three verses in the Torah ... Because of this [i.e., because the letters of the Torah also are the names of God if read in different combinations], a Torah scroll that has a single mistake — even in a letter that does not change the meaning of a word and that seems to be superfluous — is unfit for use ... It was this that brought the Sages to record all of the full and defective spellings in the Torah and Sacred Writings and to write books recording this tradition up to the time of Ezra ha-Sofer who exerted himself greatly in this matter ... and it would seem that the Torah written as a black fire atop a white fire was written without interruptions between the letters so that it could be read as the names of God or in the manner in which we read it which recounts the mitzvos. It was given to Moshe [to be written] separated into words which reveal the mitzvos while at the same time he received it orally in the manner which reveals the names of God.

Thus, when God dictated the Torah to Moshe, He commanded him to stop his transcription between various letters, words and sentences. These pauses serve to enable us to understand the mitzvos.

At that time, He also commanded Moshe to make emendations to the text which are referred to as *tikkunei soferim*. In the verse (ibid. 18:22) he was to write AND AVROM WAS STILL STANDING BEFORE GOD rather than AND GOD WAS STILL STANDING BEFORE AVRAHAM as was written in God's Torah. In the verse (*Bemidbar* 12:12) he was to write WHEN HE LEAVES HIS MOTHER'S WOMB, HALF HIS FLESH IS CONSUMED rather than WHEN WE LEAVE OUR MOTH-ER'S WOMB, HALF OUR FLESH IS CONSUMED. These emendations were made to the text so that people could be taught the literal meaning of the verses, while their great Sages would be able to understand the deep secrets that are alluded to in the manner in which the Torah was written before God [i.e., without the tex-tual emendations].

Moshe was also given all of the instances where the spelling and reading of words differ [*kri* and *ksiv*] as well as the voweli-zation and cantillation notes [both of which serve as a means of punctuation] so that the meaning of the words and the mitzvos would be understandable. Although it would have been clearer if Moshe had written these in his *sefer* Torah [instead of passing them down orally], he was not permitted to do so, for in this way the text of the Torah includes many additional meanings. As R. Natronai Gaon wrote: The vowels and notes of the Torah limit the interpretations. The only changes that Moshe was per-mitted to make from the text that he saw as a black fire atop a white fire [with the exception of the *tikkunei soferim*] were the separation of the letters into words, sentences, portions and books.

THE MESORES

The Talmud (*Eruvin* 13a) records:

> When I [R. Meir] came to R. Yishmael, he asked me: "My son, what is your profession?" I told him: "I am a scribe." He said: "My son, be careful in your work, for your profes-sion is the work of heaven. If you omit a single letter or

*add a single letter [to the Torah] you will end up destroy-
ing the entire world."*

We see that the halachos pertaining to writing a Torah scroll
are so important that the Talmud sees fit to warn scribes that a
single error in a single letter can bring destruction to the world.
It was for this reason that the Sages in the generations until
Ezra the Scribe were exceedingly careful in their transcriptions
— transcriptions which became known as the *mesores* [literally,
tradition]. The Sages who lived afterwards [who no longer had
access to men with prophetic vision like Ezra and his col-
leagues] composed books — the *Mesorah ha-Gedolah* and the
Mesorah ha-K'tanah — in which they recorded all of the instances where words are written in full or deficient form, with
dots above the letters, or with smaller or enlarged letters. They
also noted the beginnings and ends of sentences and portions as
well as the number of crowns that are to be placed above certain
letters.

A number of works from Talmudic times that record the *mesores* were composed and remain extant, including the minor
tractates *Soferim* and *Sefer Torah* [found in most editions of the
Talmud after tractate *Avodah Zarah*], *Midrash Chaseros ve-
Yeseiros* and *Midrash Tagin*. Rambam, in his *Yad ha-Chazakah*,
deals with the *mesores* of *sifrei Torah* extensively and devoted
much effort to clarifying the myriad details. He writes (*Hilchos Sefer Torah 8:4*):

> *And the work upon which we based ourselves in these
> matters [in establishing the correct text] is the well known
> sefer in Egypt that contains the twenty-four books [of Tan-
> ach] that had been in Jerusalem for many years and was
> used to correct [other] scrolls. And they relied upon it to
> check scrolls because it had been checked by Ben Asher ...
> and I relied upon it for the sefer Torah which I wrote.*

The *mesores* also includes six types of divisions which Moshe

used in the *sefer Torah* that he wrote: the separation of the Torah into five books, the separation between various *parshiyos*,
the amount of space to be left between words, between letters,
between lines and between the stanzas in *shiras ha-yam* (Shemos
15:1-19) and in *shiras ha-azinu* (Devarim 32:1-43). Each one of these
separations is made by leaving an apropriate amount of space.

LATER DIVISIONS

The division of the Torah into *sedarim* [the portions read on
Shabbos] — e.g., *Bereishis, Noach, Lech Lecha* et. al. — is of later
origin and was made by the early Sages so that there would be a
set portion to be read each Shabbos.

The division of each *sidrah* into *aliyos* [the seven individual
portions into which each *sidrah* is divided and for which different people are called up to the Torah] has no firm basis in halachah, but was established by a scholar as a guide for the reader to
know where to stop. Different divisions may be used for the
aliyos as long as they conform with the halachic guidelines
brought in Shulchan Aruch that detail the minimum amount
of verses for each *aliyah* et. al. [see *Shulchan Aruch, Orach
Chaim* 137-138].

The present division of the Torah [and *Nach*] into *perakim*
[chapters] is not of Jewish origin and often contradicts the *mesores* and its division of *Tanach* into *parshiyos*.

THE PARSHIYOS

The five books of the Torah are divided into six hundred and
sixty-nine *parshiyos* [chapters] which are indicated in the Torah
by leaving a space equivalent to nine letters. All the material
until the space forms one chapter, all the material afterwards
forms the next chapter. When God dictated the Torah to Moshe,

He paused between each chapter to give Moshe an opportunity to reflect upon what had been said before he would hear new material. Just as there was a time interval between the dictation of each *parashah*, so too was Moshe commanded to leave a physical space between each *parashah*.

The *parshiyos* vary greatly in length: some contain tens of verses while others consist of a single verse. If the *parashah* is extremely short, we understand that it contains many oral teachings which need time for reflection. In some instances, the brevity of the *parashah* is an indication that its subject differs greatly from that following and that no inferences should be made from their juxtaposition. Some *parshiyos* are extremely long indicating that the subjects are a single theme. Sometimes, the *parashah* is long because the Torah "speaks as man would speak" as in the case of the *tochachah* [the portion of reproof] in *Devarim* (28:15-68).

The six hundred and sixty-nine *parshiyos* of the Torah are divided into two forms: *stumos* — closed *parshiyos* — and *petuchos* — open *parshiyos*. The former means that there is a connection between the subjects of the two *parshiyos* while the latter indicates that there is no connection. In both cases, a space equivalent to nine letters is left between each *parashah*. However, there is a difference of opinion as to how one is to indicate the division. Our practice is to begin an open *parashah* on a new line while *a parashah s'tumah* is indicated by beginning the new *parashah* immediately following the nine blank spaces, even on the same line.

In printed *chumashim*, a *parashah s'tumah* is indicated by the letter *samech* while a *parashah petuchah* is indicated by the letter *peh*. If the new *parashah* also begins a new *sidrah*, the letter *peh* or *samech* is repeated three times. In Torah scrolls, there is no difference between *parshiyos* in the middle of a *sidrah* and those that mark the beginning of a new *sidrah*.

Many of the *parshiyos* in the Torah are not recorded in the order in which they occurred. In most of the places where we find *parshiyos* that do not follow the chronology of events, the Sages offered reasons for the change. Thus, for example, the Talmud (*Shabbos* 115b-116a) notes that the *parashah* of *vay'hi bin'soa* (*Bemidbar* 10:35-36) should have been recorded in the beginning of *Bemidbar* where the Torah talks about the encampment of the Jews in the wilderness. It was recorded in its position so as to separate two other *parashiyos* that detail punishment. There are numerous other instances where the chronology of events is not followed and no reason is offered as to why the Torah chooses to depart from the order that events transpired. The Sages, recognizing that there are reasons that are known only to He who gave the Torah, declared that *ein mukdam u'm'uchar baTorah* — there is no chronological sequence in the Torah.

THE LETTERS OF THE TORAH

There are sixteen letters in the Torah that are written in variant form: ten of them are enlarged and six of them are smaller than usual. The ten enlarged letters are:

1. The *beis* of *bereishis* (*Bereishis* 1:1).
2. The *nun* in *notzer* (*Shemos* 34:7).
3. The *reish* in *acheir* (ibid.).
4. The *vav* in *gachon* (*Vayikra* 11:42).
5. The *gimel* in *ve-hisgaleach* (ibid. 13:33).
6. The *yud* in *yigdal* (*Bemidbar* 14:17).
7. The *ayin* in *shema* (*Devarim* 6:4).
8. The *daled* in *echod* (ibid.).
9. The *lamed* in *vayeshalchem* (ibid. 29:27).
10. The first *heh* in *ha'loh* (ibid. 32:6).

The six letters that are written smaller than usual are:

1. The *heh* in *behi'bar'am* (*Bereishis* 2:4).
2. The *kaf* in *liv'kosah* (ibid. 23:2).
3. The *kuf* in *katzti* (ibid. 27:46).

4. The *aleph* in *vayikra* (*Vayikra* 1:1).

5. The *mem* in *mokdah* (ibid. 6:2).

6. The *yud* in *teshi* (*Devarim* 32:18).

There are a number of other letters which are written in an unusual way: e.g., the upside down *nun* which is placed before and after the *parashah* of *vay'hi bin'soa* (op. cit.). These variations — referred to as *iturei soferim* [literally, scribal crowning] — were passed down by scribes from generation to generation from the time of Ezra and before that to Moshe. Some of these variations have been lost because of the need to write many scrolls and to rely upon scribes who did not have a tradition dating back to Moshe. They therefore based their scrolls on those laws which are specifically mentioned in halachic literature. Rambam (*Hilchos Sefer Torah* 7:11) writes that the only variations that are halachically obligatory are the transcription of words in either the *malei* — full — or *chaser* — deficient — forms.

There are ten places in the Torah where dots are placed above the letters:

1. In the dialogue between Sarah and Avraham (*Berishis* 16:5), a dot is placed over the second *yud* in the word *beinecha*.

2. In the dialogue between the messengers of God and Avraham (ibid. 18:9), dots are placed above the letters *aleph*, *yud* and *vav* in the word *eilav*.

3. In the incident of Lot and his daughters (ibid. 19:33), a dot is placed over the second *vav* in the word *uv'kumah*.

4. In the meeting between Yaakov and Esav (ibid. 33:4), dots are placed above the letters of the word *va-yishakeyhu*.

5. When the verse talks about the sons of Yaakov going off to tend their flocks (ibid. 37:12), dots are placed over the letters in the word *es*.

6. In the census of the Levites (*Bemidbar* 3:39), dots are placed over the letters of Aharon's name.

7. In the *parashah* that teaches us the laws of the *Pesach sheni* (ibid. 9:10), a dot is placed over the *heh* in the word *rechokah*.

8. In the recounting of the war with Sichon (ibid. 21:30), a dot is placed over the *reish* in the word *asher*.

9. In the portion detailing the laws of the sacrifices of Sukkos (ibid. 29:15), a dot is placed over the second *vav* in the word *v'isaron*.

10. In the verse in which Moshe tells Israel that the concealed parts of the Torah remain God's (*Devarim* 29:28), eleven dots are placed over the words *lanu u'levaneinu*.

The Sages explain that the dots over the letters come to teach us lessons that could not be derived from the text itself.

Seven letters — *shin, ayin, tes, nun, gimel* and *tzadi* — have a crown consisting of three points on their tops. Six other letters — *beis, daled, kuf, ches, yud* and *heh* — have a crown with a single point. The letters *mem, lamed, aleph, chaf, sof, samech, vav, peh* and *reish* are written without crowns. The crowns on the letters are called *tagin*.

Many deductions were made based on the *tagin* above the letters. Thus, we find the following in the Talmud (*Menachos* 29b):

R. Yehudah taught in the name of Rav: When Moshe ascended to the firmament, he found the Holy One, blessed is He, sitting and afixing crowns to the letters. He [Moshe] said: "Master of the World! Who forces You to do this?" God replied: "There is a man who will be [born] in a number of generations, and Akiva ben Yosef is his name. And he will deduce hills of halachos from each thin line."

THE CANTILLATION SYMBOLS AND VOWELS

The *trop* — cantillation notes — of the Torah were given to Moshe by God and serve as a means of explaining the Torah.

The verse (*Nechemiah* 8:8) states: AND THEY READ FROM THE BOOK OF THE TORAH OF GOD EXPLICITLY AND WITH FULL COMPREHENSION AND THEY UNDERSTOOD THE READING. The Talmud (*Yerushalmi, Megillah* 4:1) expounds: WITH FULL COMPREHENSION — this refers to the cantillation notes. When God gave Moshe the Torah together with all of the principles and details that all of the halachos are dependent upon, He also gave him the cantillation notes which are a foundation for understanding the literal meaning of the verses.

In earlier generations, these notes were taught to people by intoning them together with hand motions, like a conductor uses his hands to direct singing. The notes themselves were not written down. According to R. Yehudah ha-Levi (*Kuzari* III), Ezra and the members of the Great Assembly wrote these notes in their Torah scrolls just as they included the vowel symbols which are also a halachah handed down from Moshe at Sinai.

Others maintain that the vowel symbols were already known at the time of Adam while some are of the opinion that they date from the time of Avraham.

Ibn Ezra writes that any explanation of the Torah that is not consistent with the explanation implied by the cantillation notes should not be accepted or listened to.

As we have already noted, R. Natronai Gaon writes: Why do we not use vowels in the Torah? Because the vowels limit the explanations. The Torah has "seventy faces" — i.e., the text can be explained in a number of different ways which includes interpretations that are not necessarily consistent with the traditional vowelization.

THE DIVISION OF TANACH INTO CHAPTERS

As we previously mentioned, the present division of Tanach

into *perakim* — chapters — is not of Jewish origin. Indeed, the chapter divisions often contradict Jewish tradition and the accepted interpretations. In numerous instances, the division into chapters defies logical explanation and can even lead people to misunderstand the literal meaning of Scripture. It is therefore clear that we are not permitted to base ourselves on this division in any matter of consequence.

If this is true, how did this division came into use in the works that we use? It would seem that the first Jewish publishers who printed Tanach followed the chapter divisions which had already appeared in the Bibles published by gentile printers. They did this because Jewish scholars were often forced to participate in debates with Christians who would quote extensively from Scripture, using the chapter and sentence divisions which had been printed in their Bibles. By using the same chapter divisions, the Jewish participants in these debates were able to easily respond to all questions raised.

It is not clear who was responsible for this division. Some maintain that it was Cardinal Hugo di St. Caro (1200-1263) while others maintain that it was the Archbishop of Canterbury Stephen Langton (13th century). In 1438, R. Yitzchak bar Nasan used this chapter division in his *Meir Nativ* — the first concordance of *Tanach* — which he published to make it easier for Jewish scholars to reply to their Christian antagonists.

In a work entitled *Masores ha-Torah*, R. Pinchas Finfer of Vilna quotes a R. Shlomo ben Yishmael who wrote:

> These are the divisions of the gentiles which are called ca-pitulis ... and we have copied them so that one might re-spond quickly to their questions. For they pose questions to us every day regarding our faith and our Torah and of-fer proof [for their contentions] from verses from the To-rah, Nevi'im or other sources saying: Read such and such a Book, in verse so and so, capitul so and so. And we are

not aware of [the division according to] capitul so as to be able to respond quickly. I have therefore copied them.

The author of *Masores ha-Torah* goes on to explain:

When the Mikraos Gedolos was printed in Venice (1525), the proofreader, R. Yaakov ben Chaim, apoligized for having followed the Roman priest [Cardinal Hugo di St. Caro], and wrote: Had it not been for the concordance which had been written by a contemporary scholar by the name of Yitzchak [ben] Nasan which had already been published in our print in Venice, it would have been impossible to proofread ... and I was forced to use the chapter divisions that are brought in the work of R. Yitzchak Nasan.